J. C. Laffin

HIS WORD *Through* PREACHING

*"But hath in due times manifested his
word through preaching, which is committed unto me, according to the commandment of God our Saviour."*

TITUS 1:3

HIS WORD

Through

PREACHING

GERALD KENNEDY

HARPER & BROTHERS PUBLISHERS
NEW YORK   LONDON

This is for Mary

CONTENTS

vii

PREFACE

A Church of England bishop once remarked that a sermon is something a clergyman will cross the continent to deliver, but will not cross the street to hear. Probably no preacher will fail to understand the meaning of that, for we are notoriously critical and difficult to please when we are members of a congregation.

To a very large extent, a discussion of preaching may expect to be confronted with the same critical reluctance on the part of the clergy. No two men ever see their profession in quite the same light, and the wide gaps, the misinformation, and the misinterpretations of the writer are all apparent to every reader. Why, then, does anyone have the courage to lecture on the subject, or write about it?

For one thing, the very disagreements contain values in that they sharpen our attitudes toward preaching. But more than that, if a man deals with his work lovingly, all of us will be helped by the spirit if not by the actual treatment of the subject. When I was invited to teach homiletics at the Pacific School of Religion some years ago, I talked with Dr. Carl Patton, who had retired because of illness. When I asked him what advice he could give a man who knew nothing about teaching preaching, he replied, "I've decided that if they can preach, they can preach, if they can't, they can't, and there is nothing you can do about it." That was not too helpful and apparently seeing my rather troubled expression, he went on: "But there is one thing a teacher of homiletics ought to do; and that is to make his students want to be the best preachers possible."

I have never ceased to give thanks that God called me to the greatest job in the world. The ministry to me is the fulfillment of a promise, and I feel sorry for every man who cannot share it. Without any expectation that the information in these pages may be of great practical help to anyone, but with the hope that there is something contagious in joy, I have taken the liberty of discussing my favorite subject: the preaching of the Word.

In nearly every case, books on preaching deal only with the technique of sermon construction. We leave the content of the message to the theologians who write their books without being concerned primarily with the delivery of the message. The written sermon deals with the organization of the sermon as well as the message, it is true. But the sermon message is usually fragmentary so far as the whole Christian emphasis is concerned. It has seemed to me, therefore, that there is a place for bringing together the method and the message. For the nature of the Gospel has implications for the manner of its presentation. Perhaps there will be value in considering, in terms of a closer unity, what we have to say and the way we ought to say it.

GERALD KENNEDY

PART ONE

THE METHOD: DISCIPLINE AND ART

I

WE ARE AMBASSADORS

*". . . as though God were in-
treating by us."*
II Corinthians 5:20

Preaching has been through a time of troubles during the past years, and as severely tested as at any time in the whole history of Christianity. Protestantism has felt this upheaval more than other branches of the Christian Church, because Protestantism has given more hostages to preaching. The Bible and the preached word have been foundations of our tradition, which has made it very serious when there have been many voices proclaiming that the foundations, at least the preaching one, will no longer hold up the structure.

Even when Phillips Brooks wrote his famous lectures on preaching in 1893, he found it necessary to say that nothing could ever take the place of preaching, because of the personal element within it. For at that time, there were those who questioned whether this activity had any future or not. As a matter of fact, ever since the time when the Apostle Paul spoke about "the foolishness of preaching," there have been prophets predicting its early demise. That anything much can be expected from ordinary men talking week after week has never seemed reasonable to many critics of the Church.

It is not to be wondered that a barrage of criticism has been loosed in our time, for obviously something has been wrong. In spite of the fact that statistically the Church continues to more than hold its own, there has been a lack of vitality within it that is obvious to any observer. "Can these bones live?" is a question which Ezekiel asked, and the question is appropriate now. The answer to many has seemed to be that

3

the bones could live only if we found a substitute for preaching.

We have, therefore, listened with interest to the worship experts who have said that if more emphasis were placed on learning how to worship and the providing of worshipful sanctuaries, we could be revived. We have been convinced for a time by the claims of religious educators and we have learned much from them. Now we are to be saved by visual education. The making of the Church into a social center, where all ages would feel like spending their spare time in social activity, has been tried in certain places. The radio was regarded by some as a welcome substitute for a local congregation with a man in the pulpit. None of these things can be dismissed for all of them have made valuable additions to the effective work of the Protestant Church. But none of them has shown itself capable of being a substitute for preaching.

Now it becomes increasingly clear that there is a kind of preaching which has no power and no value. That, however, has always been true and is simply an example of a great function being inadequately carried out. But there has never been a time when great preaching was more needed than in this period of radio, movies, and books. For with the development of means for communicating, we have so little worth communicating. We are, as Shaw said of Henley, a generation with tremendous powers of expression, and nothing worth expressing. In the midst of these contemporary clamors, the world needs preachers.

The modern methods which enable us to disseminate information to every home also make it possible to control the vast networks of information. One of the dangerous developments is a growing monopoly of news sources and the increasing power of small groups to decide who shall have access to the air. The local person soon learns that he is on the radio under sufferance and that he will be taken off or moved aside whenever a network show wants the time. There is a growing number of American towns and cities with only one newspaper or a single ownership of papers. In many a community, the pulpit represents the most important remaining platform where a man knows that he can speak his word without being censored or forbidden. At the present moment it would seem that instead of the modern world finding substitutes for preaching, its need for preaching is, and will be, a growing one.

This rediscovery of the central importance of preaching comes not only from the so-called practical men of the Church but from the theologians as well. Barth may be cited as an example, and while many will regard his position as extreme in some respects, he has had a considerable influence on modern theological thought. The Barthian emphasis has helped us to understand that preaching cannot be eliminated from Christianity without Christianity's losing its essential quality and its true nature. The idea of a poem can be put into prose, but it is no longer the same thing. For the poem is not just an idea but a living spirit which is dependent on its form for its emotional power. So Christianity, because of its nature, is dependent on preaching, which as Phillips Brooks said "is the bringing of truth through personality." [1]

St. Paul writes to the Romans: "How then shall they call on him in whom they have not believed? and how shall they believe in him whom they have not heard? and how shall they hear without a preacher?" [2] It is perhaps too strong a statement to say that this has been rediscovered, for indeed it was never entirely lost. But this truth shines with new brilliance today.

What Preaching Is Not

Like every other really important thing in life, preaching is difficult to define. It is much easier to state what it is not,

---

1 Brooks, *Lectures on Preaching,* Dutton, 1893, 5.
2 Romans 10:14.

and perhaps that is the best way to begin. Before we can come to the unique quality of it, we must clear away a certain amount of misunderstanding and half truth. The pulpit becomes a neutral, relatively harmless place when the clear understanding of the preacher's task is lost. It is then that the cynic can say of a certain man that he is a first-rate preacher because he does comparatively little harm.

For one thing, preaching is not merely education, though I hasten to add that any self-respecting preacher will certainly aim at educating his congregation, since that is a significant part of his function. That is, he will supply the people with certain facts and ideas which will to some extent, at least, affect their outlooks and their living. The preacher will learn how to present controversial matters in such a way as to win a hearing before the mind can close and keep them out. But preaching is much more than presenting facts with the vain hope that people will outgrow their paganism and become more Christian through knowledge alone. Compulsory free "education" is a fine thing, but it will not make the City of God out of Public School No. 26.[3] Nor will it transform a congregation of worldlings into saints.

Preaching is not the delivering of an essay in which one gives his comments on life and passing events, though he can hardly preach without doing that. It is something beyond the authority of the speaker and makes a claim that the essayist will not make. While there are times when every preacher must say, "I have no commandment of the Lord: but I give my judgment, . . ."[4] woe unto the man who can never say anything beyond that.

It is not a theological lecture though the sermon must contain theology and should be theologically sound. Doctrine must be present but not as an end in itself. The sermon is not a discussion of morals though it will not lack moral

---

[3] Barzun, *Teacher in America,* Little, Brown, 1945, 8.
[4] I Corinthians 7:25.

teaching. It is not just a discussion of political or social matters. It is not only international pronouncements, though in
modern times you can hardly preach five minutes without
the whole world's coming into it. It is not urging a particular
program of reform nor championing any human solution.
Yet the preacher cannot keep silent when a moral choice is
before his people. The sermon must be more than a literary
production which brings pleasure to the aesthetic tastes of
men. The preacher is in a different category from the lecturer,
who may do little more than propagandize for morals or
virtue in general.

Indeed, many a fine, sincere, well-trained minister discovers
with the passing years that something is missing, and indeed
it has always been missing. Like the Rich Young Ruler he
finally turns to Jesus in despair and asks: "What lack I yet?"
It is not too difficult to determine what preaching is not, but
it is extremely difficult to define the essential heart of it. It
is the same mystery that so confused the learned Nicodemus,
for finally, it is the gift of the Spirit. But precisely because
we cannot say it, we are urged irresistibly to build a bridge
of words between the experience and the mind. And every
attempt is of some value, even in its failure.

The Unique Quality

Let us turn to the Scriptures, for the great thing about the
Bible is its ability to say for us what we cannot find words
to say for ourselves. How often, after we grope about in the
modern vocabularies, we find at last that a Biblical writer
came the closest to giving a satisfying statement about the
mysterious dealings of God with men. So the Apostle Paul,
after giving that great insight as to the presence of God in
Christ reconciling the world to Himself, goes on to show
the meaning of this experience for Christians, but especially,
it seems to me, for preachers. "We are ambassadors therefore
on behalf of Christ," he writes, "as though God were intreat-

ing by us: we beseech you on behalf of Christ, be ye reconciled to God." [5]

The Christian preacher is the proclaimer of an occurrence which was nothing less than God breaking into the processes of life to reveal Himself supremely in a Person. If the pulpit loses its power, it is always when it loses its sense of God proclaiming this Event, through a man to men. Nothing is the same since it took place, and no life can be the same when the happening repeats itself in each man's life. Preachers are not, therefore, interpreters of an evolutionary process, but messengers telling how men can be reconciled to God, who has taken the divine initiative. If the pulpit is to maintain its essential function, preachers must never lose sight of themselves as ambassadors of God.

Our danger is that we shall see ourselves as mere agents of an institution of promoters of a vested interest. In the final analysis, we are not employees at all, but unworthy voices of the living God, who "hath at the end of these days spoken unto us in his Son. . . ." [6] The preacher is not just a man with some ideas to proclaim about God or some information to impart concerning a philosophy of life. He is the agent through whom God probes and challenges. He is the voice through which God shows Himself as a consuming fire and offers Himself as a very present help in time of trouble, through Jesus Christ. Preaching is confronting man's tragic inadequacy with God's redeeming grace.

No other speech has the public and yet the private nature of preaching. Charles Clayton Morrison calls it "the public privacy of the pulpit." For while obviously preaching is a public affair, yet it deals with the most intimate matters of the soul. No other man is ordained to say the searching things the Christian preacher must say. No wonder that he must keep the time before the sermon for himself and go

---

[5] II Corinthians 5:20
[6] Hebrews 1:2.

into his pulpit straight from quietness and meditation. Yet preaching demands a response that must be sacredly private. This strange combination of seeming contradictions is one of the chief reasons that preaching is unique.

The great meaning of the Incarnation lies in its assumption that God by His very nature must reveal Himself through persons. The meaning of the great commission of Christ is that what He did perfectly, we must do with our imperfections and inadequacies. In Jesus' ministry the preacher finds his example and the prototype of his function. And though none of us would feel that we deserve this distinction, and some would have refused it if they could, the Christian preacher is nothing less than an ambassador of the God who revealed Himself in Christ.[7]

This brings us to a deeper insight into the nature of preaching. Not only is it a means of spreading information about the Christian faith, but it is in some sense a revelation of that faith in itself. The mystic can lose himself in the ocean of God; the pantheist will contemplate nature; but the Christian is confronted by God who meets him through other persons. The very act of preaching is a part of the Christian revelation. Though other religions and other movements might dispense with speakers and use some other method of spreading themselves, Christianity could not.

The great dramatist, like Shakespeare, takes us into a world he has created, and for a time, at least, we are enthralled in it. It is a real world—more real than our business and social world. Somehow we are conditioned to it swiftly and we know that, through the actors on the stage, we have for a time lived profoundly. In an even more significant way, this is what the preacher does. He adds a new dimension to our experiences, and we are aware that back of him and through him there was a power leading us into a new Kingdom where

---

7 See Farmer, *The Servant of the Word,* Scribner's, 1942.

our spirits felt at home. It was this sense of his true responsibility that made Milton pray before he dictated *Paradise Lost:*

> Instruct me, for Thou know'st . . .
> What in me is dark
> Illumine, what is low raise and support,
> That, to the height of this great argument,
> I may assert Eternal Providence,
> And justify the ways of God to men.

You may recall the Cambridge mathematician who objected to the poem because after all "it proves nothing." But it does something more than that—it prepares the heart for the still small voice. The preacher who dares to take his task as seriously as Milton took his will also be a means of grace.

The sense of being an ambassador of God makes preaching a holier experience than any other kind of public speaking. Not many of us would dare assert that we are trying to "justify the ways of God to men" as the genius Milton could do, but we are endeavoring to make people see and feel things about God. While this is not to be construed as meaning that preachers can do without long and hard preparation, there is a sense in which the promise holds for us as it did for the early Christians: "And when they lead you to judgment, and deliver you up, be not anxious beforehand what ye shall speak: but whatsoever shall be given you in that hour, that speak ye; for it is not ye that speak, but the Holy Spirit." [8] The preacher, to the extent that he is God's man, finds the inspiration and authority for his preaching in God.

Much good preaching could become great preaching if this sense of God entreating through me to you were felt. This is what brings eternity into the present and makes the contemporary word take on eternal significance. Dr. Ian Maclaren quoted the old Puritan divine who said: "When so many are preaching to the times, let one brother speak for

8 Mark 13:11.

eternity." And Dr. James Black used to urge his students to "get down deep, gentlemen, deep down." What these men were urging was a renewed realization that Christian preachers are to think of themselves as nothing less than God's envoys and to speak always under that compulsion.

Our High Purpose

"I would rather," said Socrates, "write upon the hearts of living men than upon the skins of dead sheep." This is something for preachers to have in mind. Our words, for the most part, will not be written down, and even if they are, they will have an embalmed appearance and a hollow sound. No, we are speakers directly to men, and for better or worse, that is where our preaching relationship begins and ends. No man fails to use old material at times, and many of us rework old outlines and reclothe old ideas. But to every real preacher there comes the sense of now or never; he must speak each Sunday as a dying man to dying men. Alexander Woollcott wrote of his career as a newspaperman:

> I count it a high honor to belong to a trade in which the good men write each piece, each paragraph, each sentence as lovingly as any Addison, and do so in the full knowledge that by noon the next day it will have been used to light a fire or saved, if at all, to line a shelf.[9]

The preacher's words may not even be saved until the next day, at least in any tangible form.

What may seem to many as the rather casual nature of preaching is so only in appearance. The spoken word is never casual; in the case of words spoken for Christ's sake, they partake of the eternal nature of the universe. Many a manhood has been reconstructed on the basis of words spoken and heeded. Robert Browning was passing through a London park one Sunday afternoon when he heard an infidel speaker

---

[9] Adams, *A. Woollcott,* Reynal and Hitchcock, 1945, 147.

giving his ideas. Browning mounted a bench and began to
speak to the crowd on the truths of Christianity. He had a
sense of the issues that are always at stake when a man speaks.

We must not, therefore, be influenced by the seeming
impermanence of our work. Many a man goes wrong when
he comes to feel that his primary obligation is to entertain
his congregation, since nothing much can come from it anyway. The pulpit then becomes a dinner club platform and
the preacher an after-dinner speaker. If God speaks through
me, then the moments when I address my people are moments
touched with timelessness. The utter seriousness of the occasion will never escape us if we can keep in mind that God is
offering His reconciliation to men through us.

On March 15, 1829, four days after his ordination, the
young Emerson described his purpose in these words:

> But if I can add any distinctness to your idea of God, any
> beauty to your notion of virtue; if I can represent the life of
> Christ in such vivid and true colors as to exalt your love; if
> I can persuade one young man to check the running tide of
> sensual pleasure by the force of moral obligation; if I can
> prevail with one old man to forgive an injury that has rankled
> in his breast till hatred has grown into habit, out of regard to
> the example of Jesus and his law of love; if I can arrest one
> angry sarcasm of wounded pride in the moment of irritation,
> one syllable of slander as it trembles on the tongue, by the
> memory of the motives I have called to your aid; if a sermon
> of mine shall be remembered as a place in the chamber of
> sorrow, if when the eye of one of you is closing forever on this
> world, your spirit, as it passes, shall thank me for one trium-
> phant hope—then, my brethren, it is praise enough, then I
> shall bless God that I have not been wholly wanting to his
> cause, that, by me, one mite is added to the sum of happiness.[10]

A noble expectation is surely a minimum requirement for
the preacher.

It has been fashionable in our time to sneer at Browning's

---

[10] McGiffert, *Young Emerson Speaks*, Houghton Mifflin, 1938, 30.

"Pippa Passes" as reflecting the most sentimental and unrealistic of all philosophies:

> God's in his heaven—
> All's right with the world!

But when seen in its complete setting, it is anything but sentimental. A little peasant girl with one day off a year from the silk mill spends her day walking through the streets of the town. As she walks, she sings a song of faith, and hope, and joy. The song is overheard by others and it awakens repentance, it quiets lust, it destroys selfishness, it creates love, it transforms ambition, it overcomes temptation. All in one day, a little girl's song performed those miracles. If that can happen, and it does, then the preacher need never feel that what he says is of only passing importance. As a matter of fact, what man among us has not heard some person say that something we said helped them, which at the time did not seem to us important or central? We set before our people life and death, and only a low purpose can rob us of that high office.

Discipline and Art

It is amazing how many things in life are good if they are held together in tension, and how evil they become if they fly apart. The Gospel has this understanding of the paradoxical nature of truth and the Christian preacher needs to remember this when he is thinking of his work. Men tend to picture their task as either a discipline or an art, but such thinking fails to discover that it is both.

Preaching that is only a discipline is a laborious kind of public presentation that has no imperfections and no greatness. At its best, it is smooth and easy to sit under; at its worst, it is dull and seemingly endless. The very perfectness of the technique leaves the sensitive spirit feeling that he has watched a robot perform, doing his little tricks and making no mistakes except the mistake of being there at all. Such preaching gives the impression of having learned all the tricks of winning friends and influencing people, and then practicing the tricks on dummies instead of real people.

However, preaching that is regarded as only an art, without rules and principles, becomes a smattering of brilliant possibilities that never materialize. Sermons can be like some modern poetry—beautifully spoken but mentally confusing. Like the country preacher who remarked after hearing the bishop preach, "You know, there is the possibility of a sermon in what he said," so we hear men who have had the possibilities of sermons in their discourse, but that is where the matter remained.

The sermon must have life and form, which means it is both a discipline and an art. We can learn much about the form and any man can develop the ability to construct a sermon, if he will work hard. The life, however, is the gift of God which, if He called us to this work, we may expect He will give us. It is all the difference between making a thing and creating a thing, or between being a gardener and raising a flower, and giving a lecture on botany.

Augustus Saint-Gaudens said to his pupils:

> You are not going to make or ruin your imagination while here. That is something that will remain if you have it in you; that you cannot acquire if you are not blessed with it. But here you may learn to handle your tools. So measure, copy, plumb. A carpenter who constantly uses a foot-rule can guess the length of a foot better than one who seldom refers to it.

Like the great book, the sermon is both profound and popular, widely appealing to the plain man and not disappointing to the trained mind. It is contemporary and eternal, and always it throws light on the persistently unsolved problems of humanity. All of this seems to me to demand that the preacher keep in mind that he is a workman and an artist. He is dependent on God first of all, but also on his willingness to work until what God has given to him may be given to the man in the pew with simplicity.

As a part of the preacher's discipline, it is a good thing to write. This is not a plea for manuscript preaching, nor is it necessarily to encourage the writing of articles or books for publication, though that may be good. Writing is to save us from carelessness, for the written word demands a tighter construction and a more careful choice of expressions. To write with no idea of publication but only to learn how to make our sentences stand out, finely cut, is never a waste of time. For our general guidance in this I know of nothing better than John Henry Newman's notes of 1868 on the writing of sermons:

1. A Man should be in earnest, by which I mean he should write not for the sake of the writing, but to bring out his thoughts.
2. He should never aim at being eloquent.
3. He should keep his idea in view, and should write sentences over and over again till he has expressed his meaning accurately, forcibly, and in a few words.
4. He should aim at being understood by his hearers and readers.
5. He should use words which are likely to be understood. Ornament and amplification will come spontaneously in due time, but he should never seek them.
6. He must creep before he can fly, by which I mean that humility, which is a great Christian virtue, has a place in literary composition.
7. He who is ambitious will never write well, but he who tries to say simply what he means, what religion demands, what faith teaches, what the Gospel promises, will write better English than if he made a study of English literature.

It was said that Turgenev, the Russian writer, could only write with his feet in a bucket of hot water and the window of his room open. Surely it is not hard to see that here we have implications for the preacher. The living inspiration will come from God and immerse the preacher's spirit even

as the writer keeps his feet in the hot water. But the open
window lets in the world of men, which is the raw material our
inspiration must shape. We will expect inspiration but in
order to share it we will expect to subject ourselves to as severe
a discipline as is demanded from any group of men.

A Constant Need

When the world seems bent on worshiping the men who
can do things, and when you live in a society of activities, as
we do, the man who uses words wonders if there is any place
for him. Thus when Darwin published *The Descent of Man*
at the end of the Franco-Prussian War, the London *Times*
spoke of it in these words:

> When the foundations of property and the established order
> were threatened with the fires of the Paris Commune; when
> the Tuileries were burning—how could a British subject be
> occupying himself with speculations in natural science in no
> wise calculated to bring aid or comfort to those who had a
> stake in the country?

If not openly, at least by implication, our modern society
says the same thing about preachers, which does not matter
too much unless the preachers begin to say the same thing
about themselves.

Alec Waugh wrote an article in reply to the American
criticism that few English writers were producing books
worth the reading. He said that during the war very few
writers felt like writing when England was under the threat
of an immediate invasion. In July of 1940, for example, a
writer might say to himself:

> This book that I shall start this morning will not be de-
> livered to my publisher till April 1941. It will not be published
> till autumn of that year. Of the work I shall do today no result
> will be apparent for fifteen months. Heaven alone knows what
> may have happened in that time.[11]

---

[11] *Saturday Review of Literature*, January 5, 1946.

This of course is a special situation. But the preacher stands always in an environment that listens reluctantly and often reacts with either hatred or indifference because preaching does not seem to be a crucial act. Like the New York clergyman of some years ago, he begins to wonder if after all we had not best call a three-year moratorium on the whole business.

It has always seemed to the unthinking that speakers and writers are of value to society only in the time of leisure. Revolutionary days are for the sword and direct action. Perhaps, such people might agree, the preacher should be allowed to comfort the sorrowful and encourage the defeated, but he is not to be regarded as one who performs a necessary or even important function when violence may break out at any moment. The record, however, says something quite different. Read again the brave sermons of those men who preached liberty before the Revolutionary War and interpreted that event as it took place. Or turn to the Abolitionists and their fiery, uncompromising speeches before the Civil War. In the hour of crisis, the speaking man comes into his own.

It will seem poor taste to quote Hitler at this point, but we should remember that he was famous for his ruthless realism and he was interested in results and not pretty theories. In that strange collection of lies, half truths, keen insights, and neurotic madness called *Mein Kampf,* Der Fuehrer wrote:

> I know that one is able to win people far more by the spoken than by the written word, and that every great movement on this globe owes its rise to the great speakers and not to the great writers.

In this, he was right. There have been writings, like Zola's *J'Accuse,* and Paine's *Common Sense,* which have been as trumpets calling men to the battle. But when Jesus spoke instead of writing, he was choosing the most effective means of changing men's lives and, through them, changing society. The written word is important for the record and for a more leisurely examination. But the crisis demands a spoken word, which is why the preacher must remember that he meets men at a moment of eternal significance.

Not only is the Christian preacher at home in a crisis; he is in a sense a creator of crises. A society is not always aware of the fact that it is caught in a crucial moment, and as far back as the earliest prophets, the preacher has warned of the dangers ahead and defined the issues at stake. In personal lives, the preacher brings the confusion of the soul into the sharp, clear outline of black and white. He makes the soul hear the word: "Choose ye this day." Christian preaching is at its best in the hour of crisis for it is then that it knows its own worth and significance. Indeed, when there is no crisis, the preacher must create one.

It is necessary to come back again and again to Paul's word: "We are ambassadors therefore on behalf of Christ, as though God were intreating by us. . . ." It is through the preacher that God speaks His interpretive word. It may be that Thomas Carlyle had something of this in mind when he wrote concerning the preachers of 1840:

> I wish he could find the point again, this speaking one; and stick to it with tenacity, with deadly energy; for there is need of him yet. The Speaking Function, this of truth coming to us in a living voice, this with all our Writing and Printing Functions, has a perennial place. Could he but find the point again. . . .

And the point is that God's word, if it is to find its way through the confusion, has to reach our generation through the Christian preachers who are His spokesmen.

The demands of the ministry are too great for any man to be outstanding in respect to them all. We have our strong points and our weaker ones. The patience of the average congregation is a miracle to behold, for in spite of our obvious inadequacies, they will forgive us. But when it comes to sloppy, slovenly preaching, the congregation will not prove to be so long-suffering. People have a feeling that this is one place where anything less than a man's best is an abomination unto the Lord. It may be that the congregation is here guilty of merely wanting something to be proud of, but I prefer to believe that its instinct is right, and that the careless preacher is pleasing to neither God nor man.

This leads us to the very practical consideration of a man's future in the ministry. If you believe that a minister ought to have no ambition at all, that is one thing. But if you believe that an ambition dedicated to the building of the Church is legitimate, then it will be well to note that large churches want preachers. Not all the work of the Kingdom is done in the large churches by any means, but a denomination finds itself being judged in terms of its great voices. The Church grows under sermons, and long experience has made this quite clear to the layman. They ask, therefore, for men who can preach, knowing that with this function well done, the Church cannot fail to command a hearing, and then to command a loyalty.

This is not a new thing and it is not confined to one particular section of the country. From the Atlantic to the Pacific and from Canada to Mexico, churches with many applicants wait, sometimes for months, until they can find the man who can preach. Charles E. Jefferson remarked some years ago that in a whole crowd of candidates for a pulpit, you might not find one man who had learned to preach.

It has seemed strange to me that some theological schools treat homiletics as if it were a poor relation. Little time is spent on it, and often a man without faculty standing is engaged to listen to a few student sermons. The stress is on other things so that the student, unless he has a church while he goes to school, comes to believe that preaching is the least of all the studies. Yet when a man faces his task, he soon learns that what the seminary seemed to regard as secondary the Church regards as primary. By then it is too late to get the training which obviously the young man needs. On the whole, theological education is bringing back a more balanced program in which homiletics is finding its rightful place.

A classic statement of the whole case for preaching was made by the late Dr. Carl Patton:

> I pay glad tribute to all those activities by which the minister makes himself useful and beloved—and then I say that they are all secondary; are now, always have been, always will be, world without end—I could even add "Amen." For blessed is the minister who knows that however well he may do any or all of these things, by themselves or to the impairment of his more primary function, they can never make a minister. The church lived seventeen hundred years without a Sunday School. It lived a hundred and fifty years longer without a troop of Boy Scouts. Robert Chalmers never met a Friendly Indian. Henry Ward Beecher had no skill in woodcraft. Phillips Brooks was not an expert in the tying of knots or the pitching of pup tents. Dr. Gladden paid no attention to the finances of his church but let the trustees find the money. No record has come down as to what filing system Chrysostom used or what Savonarola did with his reports. The leaders of the Church who have made lasting names for themselves, who have deeply affected the thought of their time and made the church a real power in human life, have never done it by any secondary or accessory means; they have done it by their preaching.[12]

And while we should never assume that the man who intends to make preaching his primary aim is entitled to live in an ivory tower removed from the other activities of his church, it would be wise to read these words over at least once a year.

There are many little meetings which the minister must and should attend. But the large, silent part of the congregation he meets on Sunday morning. If he has so wasted his strength and used his time that he is inadequate for his service, then the tragedy is great and the loss overwhelming. For the pivotal thing is the worship service, and until we change the Protestant tradition, the pivotal thing about the worship

---

12 Patton, *Preparation and Delivery of Sermons,* Willet, Clark, 1938, 4.

service is the sermon. This is the place where the spiritual power is produced for the running of the machinery and there is no substitute for it. Activity is a fine characteristic in any church, but there is such a thing as going through many motions without arriving at one single worth-while goal. Who has not listened to a most impressive report of an institution's activities, and yet discovered that the life has long since departed from it? The spiritual life of a church must find its source in the spiritual power of its preacher.

In a day of movements and causes, it is one of the temptations of the ministry to become so embroiled in them that the preaching of the Gospel becomes secondary. I am convinced by experience and observation that the ceaseless pressure to serve on all of these programs is the devil's attempt to melt the preacher down for the tallow trade. If I am to serve the Master and make some small contribution to the religious life of my day, it will be through my primary function of preaching the Gospel in the church to a congregation. The most critical and potentially the most influential event of the week is the sermon.

The Church has been much influenced by men who would make it a sponsor of particular programs and a pressure group striving for certain political ends. Most churches have had at least one experience in the past years which casts some doubt on what can be accomplished by using such methods. The Church is a religious institution and makes its greatest contribution when it is a worship center. It was hardly an exaggeration, therefore, when Charles R. Brown said that the fate of Protestant Christianity is bound up with the rise and fall of effective preaching.

The minister ought to be a good administrator, an efficient organizer, an attractive leader of youth, a first-rate advertiser, an adequate psychologist, a faithful pastor, and an effective preacher—all of these things; but the greatest of them all is to preach "as though God were intreating by us."

II

THIS THING THAT IS COME TO PASS

". . . for behold, I bring you good tidings of great joy."
Luke 2:10

The Christmas story in Luke contains hymns and poetry whose origins are not always possible to trace. Of course there is the perennial debate between literalists and symbolists as to the historical significance of the events. Most preachers sooner or later get beyond the quarrels and bitterness of such debates, because they come to see that here is something so true spiritually and psychologically that the debate is irrelevant. Right from the beginning, Luke has discovered something profound and important in understanding the meaning of Jesus. In a word, it is the recognition that the Gospel is dramatic.

The universal appeal of Christmas is due to its nature as a great drama. Something extraordinary had happened, and while to the ordinary man it was only the birth of a peasant woman's son, to the shepherds it was the fulfillment of God's promise to dwell with men. After years of wandering in the wastelands of naturalism, always we must come back to this Carpenter whose whole career is a denial of naturalism. Here is an act of God that came on the world with a swift splendor that shook men from their lethargy and astounded men with its implications. It was the supreme drama, which means it was an action, a deed.

The Christian preacher is not an angel, but he has the angel's proclamation in his keeping. He is commissioned to say to men that something has happened which, though never

22

repeated, never stops happening. More times than not, if our preaching becomes dull and prosaic, it is because we have lost the understanding of this fundamental nature of our message.

What Is Drama?

A generation that glorifies preciseness and makes much out of semantics, has little patience with any subject which does not lend itself to definition. At once the attack is made that such a thing must be vague, and if vague, then of little importance. For we would rather make primary in our scale of values those things which we can define than be troubled and haunted by experiences which on the one hand we accept as primary, but on the other hand find ourselves unable to explain. This tendency to assume that whatever is indefinable is vague leads us into much trouble. For the first things are always the most difficult to describe precisely because there is nothing to compare them with, and the more actual a thing may be, the more impossible it is to say it is like this or this. No satisfactory definition has ever been found, nor can it ever be found, for God, religion, love, or man. But the reason is not that these things are vague but that they are absolutes. This is important to keep in mind when one tries to define drama. I feel that I know when a thing is dramatic and when it is not. Yet, to put it in a sentence, that I cannot do, nor have I been able to find a short definition in any book or from any person. St. Augustine said, "If you do not ask me what time is, I know; but if you ask me, I do not know." Yet so much depends on minds finding a common meeting place that we must try to at least approximate meanings.

To begin with, a drama is an act, which is to say it is associated with real life and in the best meaning of the term it is intensely practical. Once you get the idea that the thing is divorced from life and is of academic interest only, it ceases to be dramatic. This is not to say that the action must be physical, for mental and spiritual acts are as real as any. The fairy story can be dramatic for children, for they are able to believe that such things can happen. Only by making the story symbolic is it dramatic for adults, because we have lost the ability to escape the bonds of logical necessity. The historical event is only dramatic when it makes a difference to the present, or when, in some way, it is still influencing the present. The Bible is a dramatic book because it speaks to me now. Dante's *Divine Comedy* is no longer dramatic (I speak for myself only) because it deals with things and assumes conclusions which do not really matter to me, at least in their medieval framework.

The dramatic thing is always a complete thing, carrying a complete meaning within itself. It is not an unfinished chapter in a serial, and it does not have a *To be continued* as a closing footnote. If the definition of the drama is vague, the drama itself never is. It is specific and not general, and it sums up in itself a whole impression. It does for one what the flower in the crannied wall did for Tennyson. Within it there is a universe of meaning, which is to say, a meaning that is not merely fragmentary.

The dramatic thing must mean something in the sense that it will make a difference to us personally whether we react to it positively or negatively. The play which makes the man in the audience feel that however it turns out it will be of no consequence anyway is not a drama. The late Archbishop of Canterbury, William Temple, said that he was once an enthusiastic golfer. But one day it came to him that it mattered not at all how many strokes it took him to get the ball into the cup. Then, said he, the game had to be given up, because even a game must make a difference. The game champion is the man who has convinced himself that it makes a great deal of difference whether he wins or loses. If the sermon is dramatic, each man will say to himself, though not consciously, that here is something of such serious import that he must give it his full attention.

The drama always sets the particular action into relationship with the whole. The action is universal even as the tree is universal, for the tree speaks of the earth, the sun, and the rain. Through the tree, we enter the whole world of nature and finally come to nature's God. The drama does not need to say that the relationship is this or that, as the old fable stated the moral of the story. It does not say it, but the man watching it is immersed in a whole new world of meaning. The artist does it with a single object like a pair of old shoes. The preacher must do it as Jesus did with parables—finding in each life and in each incident a clue to the meaning of the whole.

Always, in the drama, the destiny of man is involved. For the behaviorist there can be no real drama, for everything has been decided already. There has to be the element of choice and the struggle of the soul. Drama demands conflict. In the case of the Greeks, the conflict is between a man and his fate, and though the outcome of the struggle is never in doubt, the man's reaction is a matter of uncertainty and hence, it is dramatic. For the Christian, there is freedom of choice and the responsibility of decision, and God meets men dramatically, which is to say, He meets them in crisis. Not all of life is a piece and not all of a man's experience is smooth flowing. Our destiny, therefore, is always being determined by a series of actions—a series of dramas.

The drama deals with the emotions and never touches merely our minds. That means that it is always stimulating. It does not hold a high tension for very long, but the attention is always on call because at a moment when we may least expect it something most important will be decided. If the stream flows quietly here, it will not always be so. Somewhere there are the rapids, the danger, and the rough water. So the

thing that is dramatic always has the sense of expectancy and
the tiptoe attitude. The few tense moments when our hearts
were strangely troubled or warmed are the ones we will
remember. But in between there is anticipation and memory,
which gives the whole drama unity and interest.

In all of this, the material defines the dramatic possibilities, it is true, and the subject matter is the central thing.
But technique is not unimportant, for the drama demands
the use of tools in the hands of a skilled man. Underneath
the whole business there are great principles which will not
automatically produce a drama, but without which it will
never be produced. Anyone who would produce a word that
will reach the wills of his hearers must at least know what
the drama is not, and then spend time enough to master the
methods of the great playwrights.

It is this dramatic element that is the difference between
a merely persuasive speaker and an inspiring one. That experience which Longinus described as "lifting an audience
to ecstasy" is open to the speaker who is aware of the dramatic
nature of life and succeeds in bringing the sense of terrible
and beautiful possibilities into a sharp focus. This is seen in
the case of the teacher. The great teacher is the dramatic one.
It is not too important whether the method used be the lecture, the discussion, or the tutorial. We have gone wrong in
putting too much stress on the method—if the teacher has
no dramatic power, nothing will help him reach his students.
It is the meaning of the matter that counts and that is found
through principles that illuminate the soul and through feelings that touch the will. The teacher with what we call "personality" is the teacher who has a sense of the dramatic and
knows how to make the subject exciting thereby.

One man has written of this experience in these words:

> For a few moments we have known a cessation of the out-
> ward life of the world. We have known an intensification of
> the life of the spirit. Everything has been so clarified that a

gesture, a poetically right phrase, a sob, seemed to resolve all that has puzzled us in living, seemed to lift us up, to glorify us.

This is the moment toward which all drama tends. This is the inundation of the spirit, in beauty and clarity, toward which the art of the theater gropes. And this, in a world from which divinity and mystery have been unsparingly shorn, this is as near as we are likely to come to the divine and the spiritual. It is, of course, the thing that escapes all definitions of theater or drama.[1]

It may be questioned whether men will come closest to the spiritual in the theater, but that we come closest to spiritual truth through the dramatic approach is right. Still, when it comes to defining it, we are unable to say, "Lo here, lo there." It is all about us, for it is the fundamental stuff of life, and only materialistic, cynical, world-weary generations forget it.

The Gospel as Drama

There has been an attempt made in recent years to throw all religions into a common melting pot and then say, "See, they are all alike. One is as good as another and none are either unique or supernatural." A great deal of our study of comparative religion has been for the most part an effort to make all religions manifestations of what an older generation called "natural theology." There are some religions which lend themselves to this treatment and suffer no ill effects. But when Christianity is so confined, it dies. We have learned, or rather we should have learned, that Christianity consists of another dimension which does not allow it to be at home in a flatland.

Our faith began with a happening which never had been before and never can be again. Its message of succor and challenge stems from that happening and its work is done in the world by preaching it. All of what we have to say springs from that, and the renewal of the Christian power for every

---

[1] Cheney, *The Theatre*, Tudor, 1939, 8.

generation lies in the story's being retold to every new generation. This means that if every record were eliminated and every preacher silenced, Christianity could not recur again. Our religion depends on a succession of witnesses constantly bearing witness to what happened in Palestine in the days of Caesar Augustus. In the words of one of our greatest interpreters of the Event: "To put it paradoxically, in happening again it would show that it had never, according to its own definition of itself, happened at all." [2] All of this means that the Gospel is dramatic, in that it centers in an action which provides the clue to the meaning of God and life.

One of the tragedies of the Church is the way the story of Jesus becomes overlaid with dull platitudes. Actually, there is no more dramatic theme in all of history than that of Christ. It has such terrific power that missionaries have told of men who have read the Gospels for the first time, and been converted to Christianity by the reading alone. It is in this power that the Gospel finds one of its chief witnesses for its truth. Professor Ernest Hocking of Harvard University once said:

> A theory is false if it is not interesting. A proposition which falls on the mind so dully as to excite no enthusiasm, has not attained to the level of truth. Though the words be accurate the import has leaked away from them and the meaning is not conveyed. Whatever doctrine tends to leave men unstrung, content, complacent, and at ease, is a treachery and a deceit. We have to require of our faith not what is agreeable to the indolent spirit but what is at once a spur and a promise.

We should not forget Horace Bushnell's wise remark that the Gospel is a gift to the imagination. We shall be wrong if we try to keep the appeal of Christianity on the same level as that of a philosophy. Kierkegaard's abhorrence of making Christianity a philosophy sprang from this same insight that

2 Farmer, *Servant of the Word*, Scribner's, 1942, 19.

came to Bushnell. Men are saved in the realm of imagination. This was always clear to the saints. Chesterton's fine study of St. Francis of Assisi points out that while that humble man was not what might be termed "a theatrical person," he was very much a dramatic personality who saw things not as a picture, but in action, like a play. It was this that gave the saints their golden extra, the indefinable thing that made them revelations of their faith.

The Church has been, itself, a great drama. Its life has not been an embalming of something that once happened, or a vain attempt to preserve itself by becoming the champion of the *status quo*. That it has sometimes done this cannot be denied, but always the sense of the past, as if it were now happening, keeps the Church from death. The secret of its resurrection power is its assurance that Jesus comes again and the future belongs to him. To use Heim's picture: Christ was the flash of the lightning but the thunder roll of God's final victory has not yet sounded. Yet, and this is the crux of the whole matter, the lightning and the thunder are not disconnected happenings, but truly one event. The Church has always had some sense of this and so it goes on through the centuries as a continuing drama.

So much of the ritual of the Church has this sense of God's action. An old Methodist told Dr. Harold S. Darby of England that during the Blitz he had discovered new help from the benediction. Unable to read for any length of time during the long hours of bombing, he began to repeat the words: "The grace of our Lord Jesus Christ, and the love of God, and the fellowship of the Holy Spirit." He found such comfort from these phrases that he was sure other people would have the same experience if they could be directed to the great words. Why is this? Is it not that the grace, the love, and the fellowship are active things which reach not only our minds but our hearts? The experience is one of going back to

Christ, finding a present comfort, and facing the future with a new assurance. It is, in a word, a dramatic experience.

Cardinal Newman had this dramatic feeling about the Mass. It was to him an action that did not loiter or move leisurely. In it there was the sense of hurry as if the mission were too awful to be delayed. Words in this drama are never regarded as ends in themselves forming some sort of beautiful pattern. They are, on the contrary, means to an end and so they come and go quickly. Newman felt that the sacrifice which the Mass re-enacts represented a work too great to allow a gradual approach. It is a thing of suddenness and hurry.

It is this nature of the Christian experience which makes it impossible to describe it adequately in purely gradual or revolutionary terms. That there is growth and development in it no one would wish to deny, but the reason we always come back to St. Paul's descriptions of the experience is because he has that sense of the almost catastrophic suddenness of the divine act. John Bunyan in *Grace Abounding* talks about finding three or four poor women in the streets of Bedford talking about their Christian experience with such a joy in their faces that they had the appearance of living in a new world. This quality is born out of the dramatic nature of the Gospel, which is to say that the Gospel is an act. It is noteworthy that the Book of Mark, being the oldest of the Gospels, reflects this sense of Jesus as God's action.

Our Christian preaching is not the reciting of a long list of sins and a long list of ethical duties. It is the production of a vision of the King who came once, comes now, and will come continually to great men or to "three or four poor women." Then the drama is repeated over and over again which is the promise of a new heaven and a new earth to men who will enter it. The word is not of that which is to be the subject of contemplation only. It is a word that probes our wills and demands an active response.

Drama vs. Melodrama

To speak of being dramatic has an unpleasant sound to many ears for it brings up memories of elocution and an old-time pulpit oratory that leaves modern audiences cold. The only way to treat that now outgrown form of drama is to burlesque and make ridiculous what once was regarded seriously. It should not be necessary to say that we do not have an ancient oratory in mind.

Nor are we thinking of what is so often called "dramatic preaching," which is merely physical activity in the pulpit. We do not mean the breaking of chairs or the tearing of hair. Nor are we speaking for the kind of setting where, by the manipulation of lights and stagecraft, some men get what they call "dramatic effects." Remember the old formula which declared that the basic needs of the drama are "three planks and a passion." As a matter of fact, if anyone in the congregation is aware that something theatrical is happening, the preaching is being poorly done. If any person says, "He is a dramatic preacher," that preacher is usually guilty of an egocentric performance.

Sensationalism is not to be tolerated in the Christian pulpit, and if there is an abomination in the modern church, it is the kind of preaching which seeks to attract a crowd, never a congregation, by putting on a show. This is nothing but melodrama as opposed to the real drama. The main characteristic of the farce as opposed to the comedy is that the farce depends more on a situation than it does on character. So it is with sensational preaching. The truth does not shine in its own light, but the shoddy message has to be lighted with the flares of cheap showmanship. The effect is obtained by surprise and by the close approach to the shocking and the vulgar. Only the vulgar appreciate it and they receive no real profit from it.

Jippensha Ikku, a Japanese humorist, is credited with a

most unusual manner of departing this life. According to the story, Ikku, when he was about to die, requested his friends to see that his body was burned immediately after his death, without the usual ceremonies. He gave them some small packets which he instructed were to be placed about his clothing before the burning. This was done and in a short while there was a series of explosions and shooting stars. The packets had contained fireworks. This may be a humorous gesture in defiance of death, but there is a vast difference between it and Jesus' "Father, into thy hands I commend my spirit," or St. Paul's "I have fought a good fight." There is the same difference between sensationalism and drama.

A petty preacher can agitate the interest, but only a truly dramatic one can exalt the spirit. Too many men who note that the worship service seems to lack the appeal of the movie decide that if they become more like the movie, they will solve the problem. Let us be thankful that a worship service does not have the same attraction as the movie. Only if the box office is our standard of measurement will we strive to have the same appeal.

When Sarah Bernhardt played *Tosca,* there was one scene in which she had to stand on the stage while her lover was being tortured in the next room. She stood with her arm against the door and her forehead resting on her arm. The only movement was the convulsive twitching and clenching of her free hand. The dramatic tension was almost unbearable. But what would Hollywood have done with that scene? It would have become a melodrama, in all probability, since with rare exceptions subtlety is an unknown quality in the cinema. Too often, instead of allowing the incident to speak its clear unforgettable word, Hollywood makes the actor deliver a speech telling the audience what it means and how they should feel. But no one is very much concerned about it because no one expects to see real drama at the movie theater.

The preacher, however, is under a different contract and performs for a different purpose.

The return to popularity of Henry James is due to hunger for a writer who can see and portray the drama of character. In one sense nothing ever happened to Henry James. His life was not adventurous from the external point of view; but few men have been so aware of conflicts, defeats, triumphs in the inner life of men as was James. His short stories are to be read by every man who wants to comprehend this dramatic understanding of life in the Christian Gospel. For while in a way nothing happens in the stories and the plots are hardly worth mentioning, on the other hand everything happens, for people's destinies are at stake as they make their choices and react to their testings.

The written sermons of John Wesley must be very different from the ones he delivered to the colliers, for they were people who were used to taverns, and cruel sports. But the evangelism of Wesley could never have been melodramatic, for he was always the Oxford don. He found his way into the conscience of those plain men of his day by his sense of the dramatic urgency of the Gospel and its exciting promise of victory over sin. The moving power of Christianity in any time and to any class of men is not revealed by dressing it up in clown's clothing but in speaking plainly and directly about "this thing that is come to pass."

The late A. Edward Newton relates that one spring when he was leaving for Europe, he left a few of Trollope's novels about Oak Knoll with his gardener. When he returned in the fall, he asked the gardener how he enjoyed the books and received this reply: "Well, my old woman and I are reading them every night out loud, and now I have to help her with the dishes so we can get right back to them." And then after a pause he added, "And they aren't very exciting either." You could hardly find a better illustration of the difference be-

tween drama and melodrama. The stories held an interest
that was compelling, but they did it through revealing the
meaning of ordinary life and not by any dependence on weird
atmosphere or complicated plot. The preacher can learn
much from this.

Preacher's Qualification

The preacher's art has its own standards and its own atmosphere. Yet it has real connections with writing and teaching.
We can learn from all of the fields that attempt to communicate truth. Louis Adamic wrote:

> To approach truth and understanding (to say nothing of
> achieving them) and, through them, to experience a more or
> less steady feeling, one must be free, intelligent, and essentially
> sound as a human being; one must possess a wide and deep
> consciousness, good instincts, intuition, a sense of humor, and
> a sense of drama. Perhaps even all these are not enough, but
> they may do as a beginning. I think, however, that the sense
> of drama is probably the most important. I believe that the
> drama of things is the truth of things. To say this in other
> words: the truth of a thing, condition, situation, or whatever
> it may be, is the essence of the interplay or interaction of all
> the factors therein which is the drama thereof. I think that to
> the extent that one perceives the drama of a thing one per-
> ceives the truth of it. . . . To write truthwardly, then, is to
> write dramatically.[3]

This is, in a sense, the Christian definition of truth. When it
is written in the Fourth Gospel: "I am the way, and the truth,
and the life . . . ," we are being told that truth is dynamic
and personal. To conceive of it as apart from life is impossible for the Christian, and it could be paraphrased for the
preacher: "To preach truthwardly, then, is to preach dramatically."

It was said of President Harper of Chicago University that
he could teach Greek as if it were a series of hairbreadth

---

[3] Adamic, *My America,* Harper, 1938. Preface.

escapes. Such teaching is only possible when a man sees that any knowledge is exciting because it is dramatic. Even morality, that dreary subject, can become a dark and daring conspiracy against sin and frustration. What the preacher must learn, then, is this dramatic approach to truth, and he must find this kindling power of the Gospel, which is perhaps the most important qualification for a preacher. The Gospel never manifests its presence in dead ashes, but in a flaming fire in the heart.

If the Gospel is true, and we had better not try to preach it until we are assured on that point, it is the most exciting news the world has ever heard. Can it be true that "God so loved the world, that he gave his only begotten Son, that whosoever believeth on him should not perish, but have eternal life?" If it is, and the preacher lets that work on his imagination, he will make theology shine and bring men to the edge of their pews in expectation. Men may not always accept the Gospel but if it is presented in its dramatic power, they will never be bored by it.

Remember De Quincey's description of a preacher who lacked this supreme qualification. He was one of those

> . . . who understand by religion simply a respectable code of ethics—leaning for support upon some great mysteries dimly traced in the background, and commemorated in certain great church festivals. . . . As a preacher, Mr. H. was sincere, but not earnest. He was a good and conscientious man; and he made a high valuation of the pulpit as an organ of civilization for cooperating with books; but it was impossible for any man, starting from the low ground of themes so unimpassioned and so desultory as the benefits of industry, the danger from bad companions, the importance of setting a good example, or the value of perseverance—to pump up any persistent steam of earnestness either in himself or in his auditors.[4]

In more recent times Marquis James referred to the same kind of preacher in the story of his Oklahoma boyhood. He said

---

4 De Quincey, *Confessions of an Opium Eater*, Everyman Edition, 28.

that, while the family was Methodist, they usually went to the Congregational Church because the Methodist preacher, though a good and sincere man, made listening to him an act of penance.

What is wrong with such men? They have lost the sense of the drama of the Gospel. They are like the preacher who was told by David Garrick: "I set forth fiction as if it were true, while you preach truth as if it were fiction." That is to say, the dull preacher does not feel that what he says is thrillingly relevant to real life. It has become a burden to him and there is nothing contagious in his handling of the Word. The celebrated Verger no doubt had this in mind when he said that he had been hearing chapel preachers for over twenty years, but in spite of that, he still believed in God.

Developing Dramatic Power

Any professor of homiletics will know how limited is his ability to convey to a student the secret of preaching power. The great reward of teaching this difficult subject comes when a young student preaches his first sermon in class, and it is obvious to everyone present that "he has it." It is not always necessary to hear a sermon—just a few words, a Scripture reading, a short prayer will often reveal the gift. Remember in Howard Spring's *Hard Facts* how the young curate gave an invocation at a public dinner, and how the girl he loved knew in that moment that he was destined for a large place in the Church. It is the power of demanding attention and creating expectation, with the inescapable feeling that in some special way God has given this man authority to speak for Him.

But can this be developed if it is not present? What do you do when you know that yours is not a dramatic temperament? It has to be said, I believe, that what can be done is limited because there is an irreducible minimum which has to be given. As Principal Fairbairn always insisted, you can train a priest because it is mostly a matter of discipline and drill; but only God can make a prophet. After we have said that, however, let it also be said that there is much any man can do to grow in imagination and in an appreciation of the dramatic nature of life and the Gospel. The first thing is to be aware of the necessity of this and to be sure that in this direction lies preaching power.

We need to learn how to concentrate spiritually. This means that we have to see the spiritual world as a real world and spiritual forces as real forces. Many a preacher is able to see and describe adequately physical forces in conflict, but the inner conflicts of a man's soul, and the spiritual powers at war, are only vague, amorphous matters without sharpness or impact. One advantage that the preacher has who believes in a personal devil is that the conflict becomes real, while if evil is only a drift or an absence of goodness, the drama is lost in generalities. When Paul describes sin, he makes it actual, as it is, and whether we literalize all the way or not, we cannot do better than to become steeped in the Pauline sense of sin as direct, active, positive. That makes the overcoming of it not just an intellectual 'yes' or 'no' but a battlefield where the clashing of arms is heard.

The Christian life seems so hard to make thrilling that even Dante could not make his description of Paradise as interesting as his picture of Hell and Purgatory. Yet the real preacher has learned that if he can make living for Christ like a great cavalcade, he has come closest to describing the experiences of the saints who chose Christ as "their Captain in the well-fought fight." To rescue from dullness and routine is the preacher's responsibility, and he fulfills it by waiting on the Lord until the drama of the situation is revealed. Many a person who would never have read a sermon has been first intrigued and then saved by Bunyan's *Pilgrim's Progress*. The reason is not hard to find—he made the Christian life a journey and an adventure.

✕   This would seem to indicate that a preacher needs to read novels, plays, songs, legends, and poetry. The kind of literature which is called "imaginative" ought to constitute a large percentage of the preacher's reading. This is especially true if the man is not very imaginative. What do the plain people read? It is not to be intimated that the preacher ought to read only that, but he ought to learn why people read what they do read, and how he can use those methods which appeal, for his own saving word. And do not despise children's stories. The great preacher is always childlike in his sense of wonder and in his sense of the dramatic nature of truth.

In time, I believe, any man can increase his dramatic power. When driving your car (preferably not in the midst of traffic) or when walking, learn to see things in movement, in conflict, in action and reaction. It may be that only a Blake can hear a multitude of the heavenly host singing, "Holy, Holy, Holy," when the sun goes down, instead of seeing merely a round shining object like a guinea. But a man can learn to look expectantly. The world and life are not made of so much dead stuff but of forces in battle array and of principles on the march. There is a story of Henry Ward Beecher, who in one of his sermons described an angel standing on the ramparts of heaven holding a spear tipped with a silver star. "How did you ever think of that star?" asked a member of the congregation. "I didn't think of it," Beecher answered, "I saw it."

→   Is it necessary for a man to actually experience what he wishes to speak about? Must the preacher be limited to personal happenings when it comes to speaking with power? I do not think so. An actor plays many a part that he has not actually lived, and a preacher if he has imagination can weep with those who weep and rejoice with those who rejoice. Salvini was often observed walking up and down the dark stage before the public performance because, as he said, "I walk me into him." Coquelin in an essay written in 1880 insisted that it is possible to express feelings which have not been experienced and which by the very nature of things cannot be experienced. Garrick once replied to a young actor who was complaining about inadequate inspiration: "If you cannot give a speech, or make love to a table, chair or marble as to the finest woman in the world, you are not nor ever will be, a great actor."

You may properly object that a preacher is not an actor and that is true. But the preacher's art is basically the dramatic art and we can learn more from actors than from any other profession. We may be sure that the truth which has not kindled our own imaginations until it seems to be the most exciting insight we can share, will never find its way into the heart of the congregation. We must wait until we have been able to walk ourselves into it and felt its impact within our emotional life. We are not ready to preach until we know that what we have to say will demand a choice, and that the choice will affect personal destinies.

But after all has been said, I cannot help but feel that the best way to learn how to preach with power is to steep oneself in the Scriptures. The Bible is the great source book of the Gospel and in it there is revealed this dramatic nature. How the Old Testament brings to a climax the great tragedy of sin and the great glory of being found by God. The Gospels move with speed to the decisive moments, and Paul makes the Christian challenge like the call of a bugle. The philosopher may become academic, but the Christian preacher proclaims a message of such urgency and with such a breathless quality that it need never be dull.

III

HANDLING ARIGHT
THE WORD OF TRUTH

> "... a workman that needeth
> not to be ashamed."
>
> II Timothy 2:15

If there is any experience that can compare with standing before a great congregation to preach the good news of Jesus Christ, I do not know what it can be. In that moment, I am sure that of all the gifts God could have given, this is His best. But back of that fine moment, there are the long hours of hard work which alone make it possible. To the man half prepared, the hour can be only testing and shame, for its glory is only for the man who knows that within the limitations of his talents he is prepared to give his very best. It is important for a preacher to give serious consideration to these activities which, if properly attended to, make the pulpit a throne.

Preparation

Because everything is grist for the preacher's mill, there is a sense in which he is always in the process of preparing his sermons. Our nets must be out always for only then can we be sure of catching the ideas and the insights which can so easily pass us by. Christopher Morley spoke of the mind's lines of tension spread out like the web of a spider. You can never tell what will fall into it, or when it will happen, but like the spider you can be sure that it will catch something, if it is spread widely. Every year adds to the range of our preaching powers so that I have never understood the modern

40

church's outcry for young preachers. A man ought to be a better preacher every year than he was last year, and other things being equal, the mature man who is still alert has things to give which youth cannot yet comprehend.

There is a kind of preaching which seems like a new house —too new and still in the process of construction. Preaching ought to be like a home where men have lived and had their greatest experiences through the years. Alexander McClaren spoke of sermons like new wine—not properly aged. This is in some ways an unfortunate figure for a Methodist, but the meaning is clear. I once listened to a man who always revealed the book he had been reading that week. It never went back farther than that, and as a result, the new book was too important and the sermon lacked critical evaluation. Said Simonides: "Give me twice the time, for the more I think the more it enlarges." Time alone can bring individual experience to its true perspective. If anyone doubts this, let him read over his early sermons.

There is a saying that "a house-going ministry makes a church-going people." If that was ever true, I do not believe it is today. How often have I heard a layman say of a colleague that while he is a nice fellow, he cannot preach, and people do not go to church. This is not the place to weigh the relative merits of calling as over against study, but it is the place to insist that calling will not bring people to church. Men come to hear a sermon and not to hear a running commentary on the headlines or a little pious gossip about what has been going on in the parish. If we are to preach, we must study.

There are two main enemies of the preacher's study—his own laziness and the trivial (though they do not always appear so) demands of people. So far as the first is concerned, if a man has not started right, he has a most difficult task before him. For to break the slovenly habits of the years is often more difficult than we are ready or able to accomplish.

John Oman refers to the old Scottish professor who said that three things were necessary for the minister—the grace of God, a knowledge of the Scriptures in their sacred tongues, and gumption. The first two cannot succeed without the third. A steady habit of at least four hours a day of study is the only foundation upon which you can build an adequate preparation of sermons.

Vincent d'Indy was outraged when César Franck made some changes and revisions on one of his quartets. But some months later he looked over his manuscript again and was astonished at the way Franck had improved his work. Immediately he sought out Franck and asked to become his pupil. "Certainly," said the master. "Come every day at six." "But," asked d'Indy, "will that not interrupt your supper hour?" "No, indeed," answered Franck. "Six o'clock in the morning." John Wesley said four o'clock.

So far as the demands of people are concerned, it must be said that they do not mean to be harmful. Therefore with tact and persistence they must be informed that if they want preaching on Sunday, they must be willing to protect a man's morning hours. There are emergencies which arise, and no man ought to be made to feel that if his need is great, he will not be welcome in his pastor's study at any hour. But it is surprising how few situations arise which cannot wait, and at last we discover how many organizational activities in the church and the community are not vital to the Kingdom of God. Until the Church learns that the preaching ministry must be protected, the preacher must learn to protect himself, for the sake of his greater usefulness. The solution may be early hours before other people are about, or it may be late hours after most people are in bed. If a man does not find the solution, God will soon know he is slipping, then he will know it, and finally the congregation will know it. If there is any substitute for just plain hard study in the preparation of sermons, it has not yet been revealed.

Some preachers know how to keep an intricate filing system so that every reference is under its proper heading. I have never found such a system that was not a worry to me, and since I cannot work when worried, I have let it go. But there are three things which seem to me to be minimum requirements for our long-range preparation. First, keep a notebook in which you can jot down the idea, the quotation, or the illustration that you discover. If it can be clipped, so much the better, though I could never bring myself to tear pages out of books. Much fine material becomes merely vague to us if we depend on remembering it. Second, keep a folder in which every idea for a sermon or every outline of a sermon may be placed. With such a storehouse, no man need face a week, or a year, desperately seeking something that will strike fire. He will always find enough and to spare. Third, plan your preaching at least one year in advance. I have learned that taking time in my summer holidays to plan next year's preaching pays as big dividends as any investment I can make. This does not mean that every sermon has to be outlined, nor does it mean that once set down it partakes of the nature of the laws of the Medes and Persians. It is only tentative, in the sense that it is there unless something better insists on being preached. But the long-range preparation is a timesaver since every sermon subject acts like a magnet that attracts material from every book you read and every experience you have. Many a time the sermon has prepared itself, or if you prefer, your subconscious did it. Such preparation will give a more balanced fare, and the meat of the Gospel will have been more leisurely and hence more masterfully prepared.

The time arrives, however, when we must come face to face with the necessity of getting a particular theme into shape for next Sunday morning. The methods of the immediate preparation are so different that seldom does one man's method prove useful to another. The one thing to in-

sist on is that the method is best for you which gets the most
results in the shortest time. The student who thinks that after
he gets into a church full time he will have more hours for
the actual preparation of his sermon is suffering from an
illusion. There never is more time, and the inefficient method
will be a constant drain on one's ministry. I cannot help but
feel that it is well to find the best method and then make a
routine of it. Sometimes it is very wise to get into a rut.

Barrett Wendell has a good word for us:

> My method of clearing my ideas is by no means the only
> one. I have known people who could do it best by talking; by
> putting somebody else in a comfortable chair and making him
> listen to their efforts to discover what they really think. I have
> known others who could really do best by sitting still and pon-
> dering in apparent idleness; others who could do best by walk-
> ing alone in the open air; others, by stating to themselves the
> problems they wish to solve, and then going about all manner
> of business, trusting from experience, to something they call
> unconscious cerebration. Each man, I take it, must find his
> own method; at different times each man may find different
> methods the best.[1]

In the following description of a personal method of preparation I do not believe there is much to be copied. Yet I
have learned from others and perhaps any bit of experience
is worth something. Wednesday morning is the time for me to
start, and it takes an event of almost catastrophic significance
to swerve me from this beginning at this particular time. The
outline is put on paper and scribbled notes, which after next
week even I will have difficulty in deciphering, suggest what
goes under the main points. Then it can be set aside until
the next day (Thursday). This getting it down is the real
labor and it takes from one hour up, depending on how
much work the subconscious has been doing and how
smoothly the thought processes function. In some ways, the

---

[1] Quoted by Curtis and Greenslet, *The Practical Cogitator,* Houghton
Mifflin, 1945, 61.

most satisfactory moment of the week is when, for better or for worse, the sermon's skeleton has been assembled.

The next morning I take the outline and scratchy notes into a room where I can talk it out loud. This seems to me important because preaching is not only bringing thoughts to people, it is also finding words to make the thoughts march. Sometimes a preacher gives the impression of having the thoughts in order, but the way of presenting them has an unfinished, almost rough manner. At any rate, it may be a good thing to try speaking the sermon out loud if its effectiveness is not quite up to par. Remember E. M. Forster's Old Lady who said, "Logic! Good gracious! What rubbish! How can I tell what I think till I see what I say!" I speak it through again Friday morning, again Saturday morning, and then parts of it early Sunday morning. By that time I am ready to preach without any notes.

It will be a rare occasion when it is not necessary to rearrange the material as it is spoken through. This is one other advantage in speaking the outline, for sometimes the smoothness on paper is not so apparent in speech, and one point does not lead easily into the next one. Each time the sermon is gone through, the preacher becomes a little more free from his paper, partly because the material begins to flow from one point to another. George Antheil says that he can compose music without a piano because he hears it in his mind. But the average speaker, at least in the beginning, had better speak the actual words as he tries to express his thoughts.

The time spent in the actual preparation of the sermon should not be more than four hours. Yet if a man decides to spend his four hours all at one sitting on Saturday afternoon, he will not go into his pulpit adequately prepared. It cannot be emphasized too much that preparation spread over several days is much more productive of results than preparation bunched into one period. The man who reads from a manuscript might disagree with this, but even he will do a better

job if he starts early. That there are great preachers who do
not follow this principle I am aware, but that the principle
is psychologically sound I am sure.

We must develop a good vocabulary and a smooth delivery,
but we need not memorize our sermons. The outline is mem-
orized and the order of the chief points, but we can learn to
speak fluently without knowing the exact words to be used
in every sentence. Adam Clark's word to young preachers is
still a good one:

> Preach from your knowledge of God and with the cloven
> tongue of fire God will give you. I do not recommend a blind
> reliance upon God; taking a text which you do not know how
> to handle and depending upon God to give you something
> to say. He will not be thus employed. But go into the pulpit
> with your understanding full of light and your heart full of
> God, and His Spirit will help you; you will find a wonderful
> assemblage of ideas—of which the reciters and memory men
> can make no use.

All of this is true, but the preacher needs to be warned against
the temptation to depart from his outline and thus wander
too far afield from the main path of the discourse. Unless a
man is able and willing to discipline himself to keep the outline as his master, he would do better to read the sermon.
Freedom to depart can be trusted only after long experience,
and even then, it is to be enjoyed sparingly. There is a possible homiletic interpretation to Paul's admonition in another realm: "For ye, brethren, were called for freedom;
only use not your freedom for an occasion to the flesh. . . ."
(Galatians 5:13)

There is what is called in the theater the "closet drama."
It is the play written to be read but not to be produced because the author has not been willing to adapt it to the limitations of the stage. Such writing may be a harmless pastime,
but it never comes to grips with the discipline demanded of
the real dramatist. There are also "closet sermons." They

show thought and literary finish, but they are not made for the pulpit and when delivered, lack the directness of truth coming through a personality. The essay style is different from speaking, and the sermon when taken down verbatim usually makes poor reading. The preacher will do well, therefore, to make himself actually phrase his thoughts and listen to the sound of the spoken word throughout the process of his preparation.

The easy speaker is always tempted to spend too little time in his preparation. A friend once said to the eighteenth-century Scotch preacher, Andrew Thomson: "I wonder you spend so much time on your sermons, with your ability and ready speech. Many's the time I've both written a sermon and killed a salmon before breakfast." "Well, sir," was Thomson's reply, "I would rather have eaten your salmon than listened to your sermon." Mendelssohn once pointed out a passage of Beethoven's which had been corrected thirteen times. The thirteenth correction, however, was a return to the first arrangement. Was this a waste of time? I do not think so. No preacher ought to be satisfied until he has arranged and rearranged his material enough to be assured that he has found the right order. For even if the final order is a return to the first one, he has learned in the process, and the material has become a part of his mind in a special way.

The Outline

There is always an impatience on the part of the artist when one tries to reduce his art to rules. Lope de Vega said that when he was ready to write a play, he locked the rules away with six keys. Such men rightly despise the mere craftsmen who insist that rules are first in importance. There is a kind of perfect mediocrity which is preferred by some third-raters over greatness with a few flaws. Quite so! And yet, let us not despise such mundane things as rules, for even if we decide to ignore them, it is best that we know what they are.

The great artist often follows the rules without knowing it, and only appears to ignore them by his brilliant variations. For we cannot preach without principles, and if we discard the old ones, then we must create new ones.

The thing that is most distressing to me in listening to sermons or in reading them, is the vast number of preachers who have not learned how to make the most simple outline. More sermons crack up on this hidden reef of inadequate organization than on any other rock. How many men one meets who are interesting, sometimes exceptional conversationalists, but hopeless muddlers in the pulpit. More times than not the reason is their failure to realize that an extended discourse must have a skeleton and that while some novels can be invertebrates, like *Tristram Shandy,* for example, sermons cannot.

There are too many sermons written like dictionaries with many interesting sidelights and important observations, but no thread to hold them together. The best that can be said of them is what the moron said upon being given the New York telephone book to read: "There is no plot, but boy, what a cast!" Unfortunately, people do not go to the theater to read about the cast, but to see a play, and people come to church to hear a sermon and not to listen to a string of beautiful thoughts and eloquent phrases. They come to hear a message proclaimed and listen to a great truth expounded.

A novelist who had been a judge in a writing contest said that as he read the new novels two things stood out. First, there was a lack of plan, and second, there was too much over-writing, repetition, and digression, "scene after scene which did not advance the story, but merely interrupted it, until suspense and interest leaked away . . . like floundering through a half-finished building in the dark." [2] This is applicable to a great number of sermons.

----

[2] Flavin, *The Writer* for February, 1946.

When a man will not take time to make an outline first, his sermon is "a knotless thread," or like a rocking horse that goes back and forth but does not advance. John Oman spoke of the sermon like a sled with the dogs tied all about it —they do not move the sled, they only worry it. Yet anyone can learn to make an outline unless all logic has been left out of his thinking. This is not a gift bestowed rarely upon the genius, but a part of the thought equipment of every normal individual. There is often an excuse for a poor sermon but there is never an excuse for a poor outline or, worse yet, for none at all. Demosthenes said, "Persuasion is as dependent upon the order of the arguments as upon the arguments themselves."

I feel so strongly on this subject because it has not been an unusual thing for some person to come up to me and say with a kind of unbelieving wonder on his face: "I was able to understand what you said and I know I can remember it." The only reason for this is that I received such a thorough grounding in the necessity of organizing speeches from a fine teacher of public speaking in my high school that I cannot preach any other way. It is no particular hardship to always have the first, second, and third points clearly in mind, and it is the greatest help to the congregation. Perhaps you prefer to have four points; the particular number may vary from time to time, though I think Finney overdid it when he included more than seventy points in one of his sermons. The points do not have to stand out, but do not despise that either. Unless the hidden divisions shine through with enough clarity so that no one will be in doubt as to where you are going and where you have been, it is better to make sure your listeners know by telling them frankly.

Some texts contain their own divisions and the problem has already been worked out for us by the Biblical writer. Thus if you are preaching on the words: "But they that wait for Jehovah shall renew their strength; they shall mount up with wings as eagles; they shall run, and not be weary; they shall walk, and not faint" (Isaiah 40:31), it is difficult to see how you could improve on the three great ideas there set forth, or improve things by changing the order. But if we are going to preach an expository sermon on faith, we had better limit the subject by setting down the three or four precise things we intend to say about it. Sometimes when splitting of the subject assumes the difficulty of splitting the atom, it helps to ask: What? Why? When? and Where?

To go from the general to the particular is usually the best order of points, for the place where the sermon makes its demand upon each man personally is the highest point. Thus a sermon which appeared in a magazine some time ago, began with the necessity of each Christian working with other Christians and ended with the necessity of America working with other nations. That order should be reversed, for no man ought to leave our service lost in the vagueness of a nation. He needs to feel the compulsion of the word: "Thou art the man."

The preacher will do well to keep his outline simple. The writer can set down Roman numerals with subdivisions under them and then more subdivisions under the subdivisions. The reader can go back and see what relationship the whole complicated business has to the main theme. The listener is in no comparable position and the over-intricate outline is nearly as confusing as none at all. It is all right for the preacher to have the subdivisions of the main points in mind, but do not expect the congregation to keep them straight.

The outline has to fit the subject, of course. The man who fears that an outline will make his preaching too mechanical and too much the same can rest assured that the variations are infinite. Here are a few simple examples:

1. It Is True Because. A proposition is announced that may be a Scriptural passage, or a theological dogma, or one of the Ten Commandments. The sermon is to be preached

because people would be helped if they believed it enough to practice it. But perhaps our pagan philosophies have blunted the edge of its truth. People need to be convinced that it is true. The outline becomes a series of supports for the main affirmation. Thus, I might desire to preach on the subject: "God Is Love." But that takes some support if it is to be anything but a pious platitude for most of my people. Something like this might develop: (a) The good material gifts indicate God's love. (b) Human relations lead us to love at the heart of the universe. (c) But finally, it is the Cross, and the influence of that Event, that gives us our final assurance that God is love.

2. Implications. Our faith opens up to us a great insight into the meaning of life. Suppose we begin with the literal rendering of Judges 6:34—"The Spirit of the Lord clothed himself with Gideon." What does this imply? Some such outline will most certainly come to mind: (a) This is the religious doctrine of life. (b) This is the way God works. (c) Great ideas are helpless until some man becomes clothes for them. (d) The dignity of a man is his willingness to clothe a purpose of God.

3. Question and Answer. We take some question that has universal meaning and we find our outline in the answers we give to it. Suppose we preach on: "What Is Religion For?" Then we might answer: (a) It is to create character in the likeness of Christ. (b) It is to give us power to do what God wants done. (c) It is to teach us creative adjustment to life.

4. Negative-Positive. Many a sermon will need to spend some time in discussing what a text does not mean. If you preach on the words: "I came not to send peace, but a sword," you will certainly want to suggest a few things that Jesus did not mean. But when you begin to build the positive part of the sermon, which may be the second main division, there will be several points to be made concerning the Gospel as a sword in the world.

5. Doctrine. We may preach on St. Paul's great word: "God was in Christ reconciling the world unto himself." The sermon might well spend some time on the setting of those words. Then it could proceed to deal with: (a) the personal experience of Paul back of the words; (b) the light they throw on the Atonement and the nature of God; (c) what the doctrine of a seeking God does to human pride and behavior.

6. The Wrong and the Right Approach. If a preacher believes that we are on the wrong track, let him list the places where we have taken the wrong turning. But in contrast to that, the Gospel talks about a straight way that leads to life. Then, in what areas do we have to change our ways? The outline is apparent.

7. Is It This? To make such a sermon textual, one could begin with the question of the Rich Young Ruler: "What lack I yet?" First of all, then, speak of the things he had. Since these things did not satisfy, he evidently needed: (a) a high purpose; (b) a greater sympathy; (c) a complete dedication.

8. Analogy. This is one of the most difficult kinds of sermons to preach because the analogy will so easily become false or strained. Usually it is wise not to try to follow the analogy to its limit. You may preach on Jesus as the Good Shepherd, for example, but it is not wise to glorify the sheeplike characteristics of men. I preached once on Christ as a chemical reagent bringing out the invisible writing of God in history and human experience. I found myself skating on thin ice most of the time. The analogy had better be fresh and, so far as most of us are concerned, used sparingly.

9. Paradoxes. The Gospel's power to state truth in unforgettable paradoxes is a good weapon for the preacher to use. You might, for example, preach on Christians as: (a) winning losers; (b) optimistic pessimists; (c) courageous cowards. Truth stated in apparent contradictions is often effective in awakening interest.

10. Cables. The great wire ropes that hold our bridges are made of a large number of small wires, each in itself weak. Sometimes a thought may be held up and supported by several ideas weak in themselves but strong in their cumulative effect. One might preach a Thanksgiving sermon some time on the miracles of ordinary experience. Take such things as: (a) water; (b) clothing; (c) shelter; (d) police protection; (e) friends; (f) sunsets; (g) books. The list could be very long or moderately long depending on how much development you decided to give each point.

The important thing is to realize that there is no idea or inspiration so great that it can hang in the air unsupported. For that which is so plain to you cannot be made plain to the congregation until it has been subjected to the rather prosaic task of organization. Many a man wants the purposes of the Church realized but does not want to bear his share of the hard and often disillusioning task of working with official boards, conferences, and committees. So many a preacher wants to go direct to his people with his idea nebulous and amorphous. It will not do. We are not only the architects who dream the dreams and draw the plans; we are also the carpenters who must lay the foundations, build the framework, and drive in the nails.

There is much to be said in favor of series of sermons. Even in a day when much church attendance is sporadic, people will tell the preacher that they hardly felt like getting out this morning, but they were so interested in the series that they did not want to miss one part of it. This will be true especially if the series rises and seems to be moving to its high point in the final sermon. This is not to say that any single sermon ought not to be complete in itself and inspiring in itself, but the series should climb.

I think the most valuable early training any young preacher can have is debating. I would make that a required part of the pre-theological course for several reasons. For one thing, it teaches one to speak for a verdict, or a decision. It demands such careful preparation that the debater is ready to answer any possible arguments that may be advanced by his opponents. But most important of all, it teaches one how to organize his material by making a brief. Then it is that one learns to make an affirmation and build a foundation for it that will hold it up. The process is one of saying that this is true, because this is true, because this is true. The whole thing has to hang together and develop logically, and in my judgment, that is the minimum requirement for building a sermon.

Unity

There is no place where preaching so reveals itself as one of the great arts as in this matter of unity. The austere simplicity which is demanded of every artist is demanded of the preacher. The great importance of the mechanical working out of an outline is due to the necessity of unity in the finished sermon, and without the first we cannot have the second. The preacher, therefore, should be able to state in one sentence what the theme of his sermon is to be. It may be added that the sentence should be comparatively short without too many clauses. This simple test will help any of us to determine whether we have attained this fundamental demand of every art. We can learn from Jesus, who taught with parables containing a single lesson. Or read Paul and note how you can quote Paul against Paul on nearly every subject. It is because he is dealing with one side of the truth at a time and comes back to the other side later. The preacher must always do that, for the Christian understanding of life is never reducible to logic chopping. There is always a paradoxical element in the truth.

The teacher of homiletics makes the discovery that even student preachers do not suffer from lack of ideas. As a matter of fact, they have too many ideas and they want to

put them all into each sermon. We need to learn that we
cannot possibly preach the whole of the Gospel every Sunday
and that we are not expected to do so by either God or the
Church.

We are not speaking always to trained minds who have
come to us for certain information we have been commissioned to give them. The philosopher writes for a special
group and the professor speaks to students. But the preacher
ministers to the people, some of whom are educated, and
some not. Many of them are tired and most of them are
worried. If the preacher is to reach them at all helpfully,
he must be content to give one single idea and develop one
thought. This is both good art and good psychology. The
very fact of unity always implies diversity, and the preacher
should not try to compress the whole business in every sermon. It is true that every sermon should stand on its own feet
both logically and spiritually, but the preacher need not
fear to speak a word today that must be held in tension by
another word which he cannot speak until later.

All great fiction must have unity; no matter how complex
its parts and elements may be, it must make a single impression on the reader. It must "see life steadily and see it
whole," to use Matthew Arnold's characterization of Sopho-
cles. Aristotle pointed out in his *Poetics* that the mark of
every good story, novel, or play is unity. Clifton Fadiman
once reduced Fielding's *Tom Jones* to: (1) boy meets girl;
(2) boy wants girl; (3) boy gets girl. This is perhaps an over-
simplification, but it is indicative of the principle which we
are discussing.

It is the effect of the whole that matters, and no sermon
has succeeded which sends men away asking, "Did he mean
this, or did he mean that?" It is not possible to make every
word and every paragraph exciting, but all these things put
together must affect people as being a most interesting affair
because it is of personal importance. It is not a series of

detached facts that is important, but the new world which all the parts have created by serving a unified purpose. In the sermon, as in painting, composition is everything helping everything else, as Ruskin said.

This demands a restraint on the part of the preacher that involves the practice of self-control. Limits have to be set and a man must stay within them no matter how appealing the land is beyond. There is always a mass of material and illustrations, or so it seems at least, that almost fit the theme of the sermon, and it takes a strong will to recognize this as a temptation. The painter has to exercise this power when he decides what shall be included in the picture and what shall be left out. The word of Lord Acton is helpful here: "Mastery is acquired through resolved limitations."

There is a naturalness and inevitability in the sermon that has unity. It flows as if, having once started, it could come out at no other place. But the sermon that lacks this singleness of purpose gives the impression of arbitrariness and forced direction. One feels that it could just as well have been handled another way, or that this idea could easily have been placed under the other point. Somewhere within the theme there is the organization that is as near perfection as we may hope to come. If the preacher wants to handle the word of truth aright, he will not be satisfied until that arrangement has been found.

All of this, of course, spells simplicity. The merely decorative is distracting; it confuses the issue and dulls the edge of the message. When the preacher has the clear vision of where he is going, he will spot these extra things at once, and he will know that they do not belong to the essential nature of his sermon. One of the best words for us here was spoken by Saint Exupéry, the French aviator and writer:

> It is as if there were a natural law which ordained that to achieve this end, to refine the curve of a piece of furniture, or a ship's keel, or the fuselage of an airplane, until gradually it

partakes of the elementary purity of the curve of a human breast or shoulder, there must be the experimentation of several generations of craftsmen. In anything at all, perfection is finally attained not when there is no longer anything to add, but when there is no longer anything to take away, when a body has been stripped down to its nakedness.[3]

Apply this to last Sunday's sermon and see where it leaves us. To strip the sermon of all unnecessary verbiage and detours is a task that demands courage, but the preacher will not go very far toward mastering his art without it.

There is some similarity in this with golf, as Ian Maclaren once observed. That is, there are some preachers below par who can speak for an hour without any idea; some preachers above par who for an hour can speak fluently on a great number of ideas; and the preacher just at par who fulfills his duty to just one idea in something less than forty minutes. There are very few golfers who are par players and there will be very few preachers who will be par performers. But we cannot aim at anything less and through the years we should come closer to our goal.

The matter of the length of the sermon is more of a problem to older preachers than to young ones. In the beginning, we are not too troubled with the tendency to preach too long. Albert Schweitzer was called before a committee when he was a young preacher and criticized for making his sermons too brief. He replied: "I am only a poor curate who stops speaking when I find I have nothing more to say about the text." He agreed finally, however, to preach at least twenty minutes. There has been too much emphasis on brief sermons, in my judgment, for briefness in itself will not make the sermon of any value.

Yet with the growing years, we shall find it more easy to preach too long. A good general rule was given to me by a retired preacher when I asked him why he had retired, since

---

[3] Saint Exupéry, *Wind, Sand and Stars*, Reynal and Hitchock, 1939.

he seemed to be in good health. He answered, "Because I prefer to have you ask me, 'Mr. Blank, why did you retire?' rather than, 'Mr. Blank, why don't you retire?'" And it is better for people to wish for a little more than to wish for a little less. One of the things that will help us most through the years of our ministry, in this matter of length, will be faithfulness to the principle of unity as we prepare our sermons.

The Introduction

In one of his letters, Dante said, "Hence certain authors in their salutations are in the habit of saying, instead of the usual greeting, 'a tragic beginning and a comic end. . . .'" You could hardly find a better description of the beginning and the ending of some sermons. It would be impossible to affirm that a good beginning means necessarily a good sermon, but it is obvious that a poor beginning may very well sabotage what was otherwise a good sermon. What happens in the first minute is of the greatest consequence for good or ill. Once lost, a congregation is as difficult to bring back into the corral of your attention as a wild steer. On the other hand, once they are safely corralled, the competent preacher need never let them escape.

There is no room for debate as to what the introduction ought to do. We are simply trying to get our people to want to hear what we have to say. The problem is to determine what kind of speech will do that, and what kind of approach fills a mind with expectation. Some of the factors in this are not easy to define, for they are the elements of the magnetic personality. But there are a few fairly simple principles which are easily grasped.

I think the most important of these principles is directness and speed. The speaker who always loses me is the one who seems to be loitering unnecessarily long in the lobby. I want to get into the main room, for that is where the real meeting is going to take place. There are preachers who give the impression that theirs is a leisurely calling and they can well afford to spend several minutes in discussing the weather. Huey Long used to announce on the air that he did not intend to say anything important for a few minutes so that his followers would have time to call their friends and urge them to listen in. But the preacher has all the audience he is likely to have when he begins, and such tactics would be for him the taking away of the little he has. People want to feel that the preacher has so much to say that he cannot afford to waste one minute in meandering about.

As I read the great preachers of the past, I am impressed with their immediate plunge into their subject. They do not wade in gradually—they dive in over their heads at once. There is something thrilling in the sudden shock of facing a great idea and knowing that here is a man who is certainly going somewhere in a hurry. It is good to begin preaching the way someone said George Bernard Shaw walked—as if he had an appointment with himself. Our appointment, of course, is with the Holy Spirit, and the moments are too precious to waste. Remember Blair, of whom it was said that he took so long to dress his sermons that they caught cold. I will go with any man who promises an adventurous journey if he will start now, but I will not go one yard with a dawdler.

Another main principle is concreteness. The sermon which begins in generalities is under such a handicap that it hardly ever overcomes it. The introduction should be precise and picturesque. The Beards pointed out in their *America in Midpassage* that President Hoover's speeches said essentially the same thing that John Dos Passos was saying in his novels. But while Mr. Hoover's words were general, the novelist was concrete and his words struck fire. It is necessary from time to time to deal with general principles, but the introduction is not the place for them. A million men killed causes hardly a ripple of the imagination when we read about it in the papers. The number is too big, too general, too impersonal. But one man killed assumes the importance of a major tragedy, especially if I know him. It is better to talk about one concrete thing than a million things which are kept general. The introduction is the place for what Harold Ruopp calls "a life situation."

Then, keep the introduction brief. All we need is enough to give a hint as to the direction we are taking, or the importance of our theme, or the reason for considering it at this particular moment. It does not take very long to show why our theme is relevant to each man who seeks God's help or wants to know more about how to serve Him. If it does take too long, we had better perform a major operation on the theme itself.

We should attempt to vary our forms of introduction. The dramatic story is fine, but not every Sunday. The same is true of a poem, or a personal experience, or a historical allusion. Our danger is to so use a favorite beginning that it loses its edge. If we are connoisseurs of the unusual or the striking, we need to be on our guard lest the sermon go up like a rocket in the first three minutes and then spend twenty-seven minutes in coming down. The introduction should always have a dramatic quality but hardly ever should it be theatrical.

Marcus Whitman, the Presbyterian medical missionary to Oregon, was a man wise to the dangers of the trail. He had been across the plains several times and he was regarded as one of the best of guides. When asked what the fundamental law of the trail was, he replied in words that have meaning for every preacher: "Travel, travel, travel," he said, "nothing else will take you to the end of your journey; nothing is wise that does not help you along; nothing is good for you that causes a moment's delay." And we who are preachers would do well to have these words in mind when we begin to prepare our introductions.

The Conclusion

Much of what has been said about the introduction can
also be said about the conclusion. That is, it should be direct,
concrete, and brief. Nothing is more discouraging than the
preacher who says, "Now in conclusion," and then talks for
another five to ten minutes. Such a man only means, I suppose, that so far as he is concerned, the end is now in sight,
but his vision is too good. If a man wants to say, "This and
I am through," and I think there is merit in warning the
congregation that the end is near, let him conclude in not
more than one or two minutes. There may be exceptions,
but they are very few.

To me, the conclusion is the most difficult part of the
sermon. If the conclusion is right, the most important single
thing has been done. For the sermon must end on a note of
triumph so that the people leave the service from the Mount
of Transfiguration. Here is the place where the wondrous
beauty and the glorious power of the Gospel message must
shine. Usually it can be done best by showing the actual
working out of the spiritual principle in a life or a situation.

This means that the conclusion has to be thoroughly prepared, and I think the concluding words ought to be memo-
rized. This is too important to leave for extemporaneous
speech, and anything less than perfection is not to be endured. How sad it is to hear a man who seems unable to
stop. The thought needs to be concluded now and the congregation will leave him completely in another moment. He
seems to have some sense of this, and yet he will follow little
unimportant thoughts down the side trails until the whole
force of his message has been dissipated. This need not happen if the conclusion is carefully prepared for then he can
stop when he feels that he ought to stop. No matter how
fluent a speaker you are, it is good procedure to know pre-

cisely what the opening words are and what the closing
words are.

Do not bring new material into the conclusion. The burden
of the message has been given and the conclusion is to point
it up. The man who remembers with disastrous results some
fine passages in previous sermons, and tries to work them into
his conclusion under what he thinks is the inspiration of
the moment, had better be warned that for every time this
works, there are ninety-nine times when it will not work.
And let the conclusion be inclusive enough to take in the
whole sermon and not just the last point.

I think a sermon should end with a short prayer. This is
not the conclusion; rather it is the quiet moment when the
preacher helps the congregation to remember the source of
every good word and every high impulse. But the prayer is
not a recapitulation of the main points of the discourse.
Let it be a quiet moment for the Holy Spirit to work his
miracle with the poor, stumbling words we have spoken.

IV

IF THE TRUMPET SOUNDS INDISTINCT

> *". . . how shall it be known
> what is spoken?"*
>
> I Corinthians 14:9

St. Paul's words to the emotional Corinthians ought to be read over many times by the preacher. After showing that enthusiasm has a place in Christian experience, the Apostle goes on to encourage plain speaking in the Church so that people may understand, and through their understanding, be led to Christ. He sums it all up in the words: "I had rather speak five words with my understanding, that I might instruct others also, than ten thousand words in a tongue." (I Corinthians 14:19) It is surprising how many preachers speak in a tongue that is familiar to themselves alone, and deliver their sermon in such a manner as to make its main thought only hazily intelligible.

There are preachers who have much to say and a great wealth of experience to communicate, but who cannot share it with anyone else in such a manner as to make it real. There are other preachers with many clever psychological tricks by which they entertain those who want only surface things. In between these extremes are the men with a deep sense of themselves as prophets of God who have taken time enough to discover how to make the message vital and plain to their hearers. Only these men fulfill their calling and only these men build the Church. We shall discuss later the content of the message, but here we are concerned with its delivery.

A famous baseball pitcher had a brother who was a preacher. They met after a long separation and the preacher said, "How is it, Bill, that after spending four years in college, three years in seminary, I get a salary of $900 a year while you, without any education, get $10,000 a year?" And the brother replied, "I'll tell you how it is. It's all in the delivery." We shall not say it is all in the delivery, but we shall insist that to a greater extent than most men are willing to admit, great preaching depends on effective delivery.

The man who comes to church today often comes without much sense of duty or compulsion. There are a few who may feel that their chances for heaven are helped by church attendance, but the average Protestant goes if he feels like it and does something else if that pull is stronger. The wonder is not that so many people do not attend church, but that so many do attend church. The competition is terrific; no generation of preachers has had so many siren voices calling their congregation away from them as we have. Some of the competitive speeches and entertainments are worth hearing and seeing. The preacher has to be good too, or he will be passed by with impatience.

I never felt such a sense of pressure as when I was minister of the Methodist Church in Palo Alto, California. At the Stanford Chapel were the greatest preachers in the country, and sometimes for week after week a headline name of American Protestantism was announced in the Saturday evening paper as the preacher for the following Sunday morning. We must not make our great calling a matter of competition, but we will do well to feel that our word must be spoken with all the gracefulness and effectiveness we can learn. If God has called us to preach, we may have faith that God has called others to hear us if we make the experience compelling.

Bernard Sobel in an article entitled "Propaganda and the Play" wrote:

> But no matter how impressive this presentation, plays with a purpose don't succeed unless they are entertaining. For repre-

sentative playgoers want to be amused; and when they are
not amused they walk out and tell others to stay away. . . .
Thus, dramatists who hope to succeed as propagandists also,
must learn first to be skilled craftsmen.[1]

It may be objected that this has nothing to do with preaching since we are not entertainers. Yet the principle is applicable to us, for we are propagandists for the Gospel and
we must be skilled enough to make listening to the sermon
a pleasant experience.

Effective speech is still the great instrument God has given
us for the changing of the world. We must not despise
delivery as being only for the preacher who wants to be a
spellbinder, or a popular preacher. Dr. Guthrie of Edinburgh
used to say: "The manner is to the matter as the powder is
to the ball." The ancient Greeks understood this very clearly,
and Cicero warned ambitious young orators that to know
how to say a thing was more important than to know what
to say. There is no possible way to speak so that everyone
will agree with us, but we ought to learn how to speak so
that people will be glad to listen, in fact unable not to listen,
even if they are not willing to accept what we say.

A few years ago, two ministers decided they would like to
have a class in public speaking from an exceptional teacher
in a church college. She agreed to give such a class if six men
could be found who would attend regularly. They were sur-
prised when it was impossible to find four other men who
would give one hour a week to the venture. While each man
had an excuse, it was fairly obvious that really they did not
feel they needed it. Some men take graduate courses in philosophy and history, but there are not many preachers who
think they need to take graduate courses in improving their
delivery. Yet many an unpleasant voice could be improved,
and many a futile kind of delivery could be bettered if men
knew how important such things are.

[1] *Saturday Review of Literature,* March 7, 1942.

Principles

Bishop Brent once remarked in an anniversary sermon
that "the good pastor is always worth listening to in the
pulpit." That is one of those pious statements that does not
bear very close scrutiny. Many a fine pastor is not worth
crossing the street to listen to in the pulpit. He may speak
comfort and strength to the needy individual, but he does
not know how to speak one word effectively to his congregation. Yet, while real masters of the pulpit are born, any man
could learn how to become worth listening to in the pulpit.
However, it does not happen automatically, and public
speech, like anything else that is worth knowing, demands
study and work. But the man who has learned how to organize his sermon, how to use his voice correctly, and how
to be content with the simple gestures which are natural
and dignified has mastered the fundamentals.

The first principle is a negative one—do not try to use
the methods of old-fashioned oratory. There is a kind of
pompous speech, full of mechanical gestures and effects,
which went out with the bustle. A few politicians still try
to use it and a few preachers think that the moment they
enter the pulpit they must speak in a sort of hollow, se-
pulchral tone. They fill their discourse with purple passages
and declaim in the manner of the Fourth of July orator at
his worst. They try to be dramatic and succeed in a performance that is a pathetic burlesque of the art of preaching.

Oratory no longer has a place as an end in itself. One of
the old medieval sermon manuscripts has instructions written
in the margin such as "cough here," "mop face here," "now
shriek like a demon." The author was consciously striving
for certain effects and hoped that the physical gestures would
arouse certain emotions. No doubt they did, but gestures,
to be effective, must be the expression of emotions already
being felt. Van Wyck Brooks said in his *Flowering of New*

England, one of the fine volumes of American literary criticism, that in nineteenth-century Boston there were "connoisseurs of sermons." They knew how a pulpit orator ought to perform and they visited various churches to revel in oratory for oratory's sake. The emptiness of content bothered them very little, for they were after entertainment and not religion. That time has passed. There are other and better places to go for mere entertainment. Those who do attend church want a man to speak the Word of God to them. It must be done effectively, but for our time the method of delivery must be the servant of the message.

Paul Robeson once said to an outstanding singing teacher: "I don't want you to make me a professional singer. Just show me how to use my voice without ruining it. I'll do the singing." This man's instinct was right and a preacher will do well to imitate him. The underlying foundations of effective speech we should study and learn, but after that has been done, it is best to let God and nature take their uninterrupted course in making us instruments for the speaking of the Word. Anything else becomes artificial, unreal, and always a little silly.

Another important principle is simplicity, which is a guide for our delivery as well as for our content. The conversational tone is always the right one, and the door of men's minds opens to such a preacher. The real artist in the pulpit always gives the impression that it is easy enough for anyone to preach. A man said to me one time that he always enjoyed hearing a preacher whose ease in the pulpit made him feel that if he had the chance, he could do it just as well. He felt that the man who made preaching seem like a specialized and difficult job was not very helpful to his people. One of my friends told me once that a woman had said after hearing a man give a book review, "If that is all there is to it, I could do it myself." He was somewhat perturbed by the remark, but she was paying the speaker a high compliment. A great man always makes others feel great, and not small. So the preacher who has learned simplicity in his speech gives the most to his people.

There is such a thing as an over-smooth delivery, which is usually the result of memorization. The discriminating listener will respond to it unfavorably and even the less critical will know that something is wrong. Jules Romains was speaking of this kind of thing when he said that mechanical speaking gives one a taste for stammering. The conversational style is not to be confused with the speech covered with a veneer of hard, mechanical perfection.

Yet a smooth-flowing delivery is certainly one of the preacher's greatest assets. The habit of filling in pauses with "uhs" or "ahs" while the words for the next sentence are being sought is a most annoying one and fatal to effective delivery. To what extent the ability to speak smoothly is given cannot be stated precisely, though I suspect that temperament and our speed of reaction has something to do with the way our thoughts and words work together. However that may be, we are fortunate if we have never fallen into this hesitating habit; if we have, we must be prepared to take heroic measures to overcome it. It may be necessary to speak more deliberately, or even to use a manuscript for a time. Very often we hesitate because our vocabularies are inadequate. To learn more words and to have someone who will ruthlessly check us if we fill in the gaps with meaningless sounds are minimum requirements for reform. Whatever it may cost us to learn how to speak without these embarrassing interruptions, it will be worth it.

The stilted and artificial style of speech is like an over-crowded room, filled with ornate furniture and artificial light. To go into such a room is a stifling experience which gives, even to the psychologically healthy, a sense of claustrophobia. What a relief to get out of such a place and breathe the fresh air of the night and look at the light of the stars.

Such is the contrast between the self-conscious oratorical style and the simple, conversational way.

Martin Luther, speaking of the people who made up his congregation, pointed out that there were doctors and magistrates who came to hear him preach. But there was a great mass of young people, children, and servants. It was to the latter he spoke, for he said that if he was understood by them, all would hear him. The preacher ought to speak to the humblest in his congregation, for if he speaks so that such a one will listen, he need not be afraid of holding the attention of the more sophisticated. John Masefield, in the story of his experiences on one of England's merchant marine training ships, tells of hearing the captain preach at the vesper service instead of the chaplain. He was impressed with the effectiveness of the captain's pointed and pithy style as against the more elaborate diction of the chaplain. Perhaps the captain was in the habit of speaking in such a way that his thoughts were communicated simply and directly. Using the same method in the pulpit, he found his way straight to the heart of the boys, while the chaplain was too consciously the preacher, using a more complicated form of delivery. Just as the Greek of the New Testament is the Greek of the common man, so the speech of the preacher is golden when it is the speech of the common man, direct, simple, undecorated.

Another principle is to keep in mind that while there is room for a decent, healthy enthusiasm, speech on a constant high pitch is one of the most tiring things in the world, and consequently one of the most ineffective ways of speaking. I have a friend who is of a pugnacious nature and always speaks as if he were shouting down an opponent. Listening to such a man, one is reminded of the remark overheard when a politician was shouting at the top of his voice: "A man cannot shout and always tell the truth." People are not convinced by the preacher's getting all worked up and being emphatic by way of increased volume. William Lyon Phelps said that there is nothing more distressing than to see a speaker or a singer getting more excited than his audience.

The need is for control and restraint, for even when a man raises his voice, the congregation needs to feel that he has not reached the limits of his power. Never should the preacher be out of control, and never should he screech or scream. There is a kind of effortless speaking which is like listening to a mighty motor, knowing all the time that held in reserve there is power enough and to spare. The shouting preacher is like a child in a continual tantrum and has the same effect on the hearers. There is something essentially inconsistent about that method of preaching the Gospel of love. A visitor called at the parsonage and asked the minister's son how his father was. The boy replied, "He is in a terrible temper just now, working at his sermon on 'Loving-kindness.'" Of such as this is the preacher who treats his message as if it were something to force upon people with sheer lung power.

Beware of sarcasm. The man who has the gift of the biting tongue and knows how to flay his enemies alive will probably want to use his weapon on important occasions and perhaps he should. Yet there is seldom a man who does not carry this thing too far if he indulges in sarcasm at all. Most people have the feeling that the preacher takes an unfair advantage when he relies on sarcasm. I have known a few preachers whose ministry was severely limited because of the overuse of what is legitimate on rare occasions. The only way to be safe is to leave it out altogether for a preacher easily gets to the place where he is sarcastic and knows it not.

The sermon needs variety; any manner of speech maintained too long becomes tiresome. There are times when the elevated thoughts demand a ringing voice, and there are moments when a man must speak quietly and at a slower

tempo. No mood should be maintained for too long, and
a good sermon will be delivered in a variety of moods. There
is no harm in laughter as long as it is thoughtful laughter.
The preacher with a good sense of humor ought to use it in
the pulpit, though always with restraint. The Gospel becomes drab when it is delivered in a drab tone. The world
never grows gray when the words of Jesus are breathed over
it, in spite of Swinburne, unless Jesus' messengers speak without sparkle or variety.

There is less and less excuse for carelessness about enunciation. The sure cure is to listen to yourself speak. If you
do not have a recording machine yourself, one of your
friends has one and will give you the disillusioning experience of hearing yourself preach. Those of us who broadcast
have learned how cruel the radio is to the careless enunciator.
We learn more when we must record a program, and then
tune it in, than all the lectures in the world can teach us. It
is then that we see how little habits of slurring certain words
or failure to pronounce final consonants can make our speech
sound crude and uncultured.

The nasal tones or the harsh qualities of our voices are
never appreciated until we listen to ourselves speak. This is
so important that every man should arrange to have this
experience, not once but often. It may drive us to a voice
teacher, and that is good. If our throats are dry or tired after
we have preached, we ought to go to someone who can tell
us what we are doing that is wrong. What hands are to the
violinist, the voice is to the preacher, and he ought to treat
it as a most valuable instrument. You only need to listen five
minutes to some preachers to know that they are being as
foolish as a musician who keeps his instrument in a cold,
damp cellar.

Yet the principles of the correct use of the voice are relatively simple. It is primarily a matter of thinking the tones
up into the head and learning how to relax the muscles of

the throat. The matters of breathing and breath control are important. Some books are helpful in this field, and a speech teacher can help a person to grasp the fundamentals in a comparatively short time. The rest is practice and study until the right use of the voice has become automatic. If there are serious voice problems, then the matter is not to be taken lightly, and self-help is not effective. But most preachers are only the victims of ignorance and careless habits.

Few things are more annoying than having to strain to get all of a speaker's words. Yet a preacher does not feel like shouting all the time, and there are those moments when for the sake of variety he needs to speak with less volume. A good public-address system will take the strain off the man who speaks in a large sanctuary. Where that is not possible, we must be sure to keep our voices up at all times so that the person in the back row can hear without straining. It is at the end of sentences that we are tempted to let our voices fall to a pitch that cannot be heard. Also, if we are using our voices correctly, they will have a penetrating, carrying power even when we lower our volume. Enunciation will be another help, for the man who speaks in the back of his throat and then slurs over his words without clipping them off distinctly, will not be understood well even if he shouts. But every preacher ought to take a personal responsibility in making certain that every person can hear every word he says, unless the person is hard of hearing.

Another principle of good delivery is to steer clear of distracting habits. Such things as pulling your right ear, or rocking up and down on your toes, or playing with a watch chain, or raking your hands through your hair do not add to your effectiveness as a preacher. I knew a man who kept taking his glasses off and then replacing them so that the unregenerate younger set began to gamble on how many times he would do this in each sermon. They drew numbers for a nickel and the closest number collected the pot. I never heard any of them remark on anything that preacher said.

These little things are harmless in themselves but they so easily become barriers in the way of effective delivery. There is probably no man who does not have some of these habits, for they are mean little beasts that spring on us while we sleep. The preacher who has developed some such habit over a period of many years is in all probability beyond redemption. But if each man is on his guard, and better yet, if he has a wife who will tactfully warn him of these matters before they have a chance to entrench themselves in his reflexes, he may well escape the grosser forms of these distractions. It seems to me wise, however, that the friendly critic wait until the Sunday dinner is over, at the very least. Most preachers are in no mood to listen to criticism just after the service, to say nothing about learning from it.

Most of us fail to realize the extent to which we preach with our bodies. The actor makes no such mistake and assumes from the beginning that he must learn how to control not only his voice but also his arms and legs. Boleslavsky was of the opinion that the education of the body demanded at least one hour and a half each day for two years. That is not necessary for the preacher, in my opinion, but arms, hands, and feet should be under control and not nervous instruments which betray lack of poise and failure to be master of the situation. Usually we will want to stand still and straight with our arms and hands used now and then for emphasis, but always with deliberation. It is not good to depend on a pulpit to hold us up, for there are times when there is no pulpit. A preacher ought to be able to stand before people and give the impression of perfect control over his whole body, or better yet, to give the impression that every muscle is the servant of the message.

Woe to the preacher who strikes twelve at the beginning. A sermon must move toward a climax which must come at the end of the sermon. That is the place where the whole burden of the message comes into its sharpest focus in each man's life. Here is the moment of exaltation which is much more than just agitating the emotions of the congregation. It is the moment of decision when duty and inclination meet head on in a struggle to the death. Here is where the preacher must sound as a trumpet with one clear call from God. It is the place where words must be simple and familiar, and where the voice speaks with a new intensity. From the very beginning, the preacher must have this moment in mind so that it comes as the high point, and not as an anticlimax.

The artist Burne-Jones said at Browning's funeral: "Much would I have given for a banner or two, and much would I have given had a chorister come out of the triforium and rent the air with a trumpet." The congregation may not express it in words, but that is what they would like to happen, before they depart.

After having learned the principles, the preacher adds to them his personality, which will create what we call his "style." This elusive thing is what every man gives to his delivery because of what he is. Let it be clearly understood that we cannot copy someone else, but each man must find his own way. It is forgivable when a young man tries to make himself a carbon copy of an admired teacher or a great preacher, but if he is worth anything, he soon outgrows that slavish imitation and walks on his own feet. Every man can learn from other men, but it is the sign of a poor spirit if a preacher has no confidence in his own power to make a unique contribution to the ministry.

I do not think any preacher ought to undertake the deliberate creation of a "style." Let us try to say what we have to say with the directness of a stone falling to the ground. If we can transmit the context of our imaginations, which have been illuminated with the light of Christ, our own style will be born. When the Holy Spirit has a chance to work on the unique qualities of a man's personality and use his gifts, then is created that which is peculiarly his own.

Style is not only skill and technique, but a reflection of a man's own inner nature and a revelation of his real sense of values. Pattison said that while you can separate some men from their oratory, Chalmers, the great nineteenth-century Scotch preacher, was not so much the orator as the oratory itself. That is true of every man who has not developed his style artificially, for when we preach naturally, we are reflecting our vision and the revelation which has been given to us. Our power to inspire is dependent more than we care to admit on our own inspiration. The great preacher, therefore, knows the rules, but more than that, he knows God. The rules become the foundations and supports for the truth which shines out of a man's own heart, and the result is the preacher's style.

Language

Henry Smith in the middle of the sixteenth century was complaining that under the cloak of preaching simply, there were men who preached slovenly. Those fellows made simplicity an excuse for rudeness, ignorance, and confusion. Yet simplicity is perhaps the most difficult of all the demands of speaking or writing. It is the unprepared and the pretentious who speak the long words and have the involved style. It takes patience and much searching to find the simple words which are the best words.

A sailor on H.M.S. *Hood* wrote to G. K. Chesterton:

Your articles are so interesting tho so hard to understand. . . . Why not come down a bit and educate the working class who are always in trouble because they don't know what they want. You see, sir, your use of words and phrases are so complicated, personally that's why I'm so fascinated when I read them, but really us average Council School educated people can't learn from you as we should . . . but what I do understand, helps me to live.

If we only knew it, many a plain man reacts like that to many a sermon.

Yet we have not really found the truth until we can express it so simply that the unlettered will understand our speech. There is a saying that if you want to really learn a thing, teach it. This means that when you have to communicate an idea to others, you must define it for yourself. We may have some hazy ideas in our minds which escape when we try to capture them with words, but until we do capture them, they are of little or no worth to us. The specialist may fall back on a jargon which is supposed to be intelligible to the initiated, but the preacher speaks to all men and only when he is ready to express his thoughts in simple, straightforward English is he ready to speak.

Martin Luther wrote in his *Table Talk:*

> I would not have preachers in their sermons use Hebrew, Greek, or foreign languages, for in the church we ought to speak as we do at home, the plain mother tongue, which every one is acquainted with. It may be allowed in court lawyers, advocates, etc., to use quaint, curious words. St. Paul never used such high and stately words as Demosthenes and Cicero used.

Like James Street's young Baptist preacher, who tried at first to show off his knowledge, we too shall find our places as effective preachers when we decide to speak simply.

John Oman quoted an eighteenth-century version of the Prodigal Son which had tried to improve on the simple language of the New Testament.

> A gentleman of a splendid family and opulent fortune had two sons. . . . I am determined to go to my dear aged parent, and try to excite his tenderness and compassion for me—I will kneel before him and accost him in these penitent and pathetic terms—Best of parents! I acknowledge myself an ungrateful creature to heaven and to you! . . . Condescend to hire me into your family in the capacity of the meanest slave.[2]

2 Oman, *Concerning the Ministry,* Harper, 1937.

In contrast to this, it is easy to see why the Bible has been the world's best seller all these years. An anonymous writer many centuries ago said:

> The written word
> Should be clean as bone,
> Clear as light,
> Firm as stone.
> Two words are not
> As good as one.

And that is true for the spoken as well as the written word.

In modern times, the contrast is brought out clearly when we compare the ritual of the church with the ritual of the lodge. Most of us have had the experience of sharing funeral services with lodges, and how any man who has been brought up on the King James version of the Bible and the Book of Common Prayer can find comfort in the high-sounding, stilted, self-consciously eloquent, strained allusions which make up these rituals, is more than I can understand. There was a time when I was invited once in a while to participate in marriage ceremonies of a certain philosophical society. In their feverish attempt to make the ceremony symbolical, they made it ridiculous. All of this is like being in a hot house filled with the sickly odor of decaying flowers. The plain speech of our religion is like standing on a hill at dawn with the wind in your face.

There is power in words but only when a man learns how to use them with skill. Joseph Conrad, who went to such pains to write his flowing English, said in one of his essays that if he had the right word he could move the world. He went on to point out that men are moved not by the right argument but by the right word. Yet finding it demands a discipline that most preachers are not willing to follow. We are content to approximate when we seek to express our thoughts. Such use of words will seldom move anything. The writers who have written for the years have searched for words as if they were diamonds. It is this sense of the need for the right word that keeps us from being like the man who was referred to by Plato as one who was "ambitious of showing how well he could say the same thing in two or three ways." (*Phaedrus*)

Irving Babbitt said that when he was writing literary criticism, he often quoted from memory, although he always checked before he published his articles. Sometimes he found that he had used a different word from the author's original one, and for the most part he could not see that it made any difference. As a matter of fact, sometimes it seemed to Babbitt that his word was the better one. But this was never the case when he was writing about Shakespeare. Without exception, he said, Shakespeare's word was always the best one and his was not quite so good. If you say that we cannot all be Shakespeares, you are right of course, but we catch here a hint as to the direction we must take if we are to be the best possible craftsmen with words.

Walter Pater, in his essay on style, said that Flaubert was of the opinion that there was one word, one adjective, one verb for every sentence and he would search diligently until he found it. His style was the result of painstaking labor. Such an approach might make us stilted and academic, if we did not temper it with the spontaneity of our calling. Peter Mackenzie was once urged to clothe his language and he replied: "Hoot man, my thoughts come so fast I only have time to pop their shirts on." Quite so, but the long hours of labor and the habits of careful speech will enable us to speak with plainness and nobility when the hurry of the Spirit's urgency is upon us.

We need to use words that live and strike fire in our imaginations. General terms have no power because they paint no picture. Government pamphlets quoting the number of displaced persons who wander the highways looking for a place to live have no ability to stir us to action. But a novel like

Steinbeck's *Grapes of Wrath* takes the matter out of the realm of the general, and we see the Joads. Suddenly we know that these are not statistics we have been reading about, but people. So the active verbs and the precise nouns awaken us from our lethargy and call for action. Let us stay away from those torpid words which, as Thoreau put it in his *Journal,* "have a paralysis in their tails." Once more we have learned how much power there is in such words as blood, sweat, and tears. There are other old words that can stir our hearts again like bravery, courage, faith, death, pain, and grief. As James Russell Lowell said, we need the tongue of the people in the mouth of the scholar.

It sometimes seems like an impossible task to preach to a congregation which ranges all the way from the Ph.D.'s to the fourth-grade child. How can one possibly provide a discourse into which the elephants may swim, and at the same time make it safe for the lambs? Some preachers solve the problem by saying that it cannot be done and therefore they must preach now to one group and then to another. Yet it seems to me that when our words are simple and living, we shall be able to tell the old story in such a way that the wise and the unlearned will find food for their souls. If we can preach so that children will listen, that is not so much the mark of immaturity on our part as a sign that we are learning how to use words as good craftsmen.

Most of us will be guilty of using too many adjectives, as is apparent when we write down what we have been speaking. This weakens the whole effect. Too many of us hesitate to call a spade a spade if we can find a dozen words, most of them long ones, with which we may describe it. The sound of our own voice and the charm of a long stream of words are the siren calls which land us on the rocks. Mark Twain had this clear understanding of the temptation of too many adjectives. He said one time that God only exhibits His thunder and lightning at intervals so that they always command atten-

tion. "These are God's adjectives," he said. And one of the
warnings on Pudd'nhead Wilson's calendar was: "As to the
adjective: when in doubt, strike it out." Much of the loss of
confidence in the pulpit comes from our careless use of modi-
fiers. It is too easy to assume that after we have found the
right noun, we may surround it with descriptive terms, and
the more the better. On the contrary, here is one of those
places where a nice sense of discrimination is most needed.

Remember the lines Oliver Wendell Holmes wrote about
Channing, who trained more men of letters than any other
teacher of his time:

> Channing, with his bland, superior look,
> Cold as a moonbeam on a frozen brook
> While the pale student, shivering in his shoes,
> Sees from his theme the turgid rhetoric ooze.

The swing from the empty, pompous rhetoric of Boston orators to the flowering of New England in literature was helped
when men got over this horrible disease of too many adjectives.

So far as slang is concerned, the answer to the problem is
summed up in one word: Don't. We can serve the community
to some extent by keeping the English language up to par.
It is an atrocious thing to hear a preacher using the language
of the gutter in order to be popular. Such men are very stupid
not to know that even people who use slang in excess themselves resent it very much when their minister uses it in the
pulpit. The good taste of people is one of the delightful
things about living, and just as most men resent the off-color
story in the public speaker, so people want to hear good
English in the pulpit. There are a few times when a slang
expression may be used deliberately. I have sympathy for the
preacher who referred to the liquor business as "a lousy business." But when slang becomes the usual form of speech by
the preacher, it is an abomination unto God and man.

When Beza said of John Calvin, "Every word weighed a pound," he was paying tribute to a fine sensitivity to the importance of words. Perhaps it will be well if we adopt some mechanical means of learning new words and finding the exact meanings of the old ones. Of one thing we can be sure, and that is that the preacher who is careless in his speech will never wield great power in his preaching. Words are the weapons of our warfare and we must keep them sharp. Remember what Sterne wrote in *Tristram Shandy*:

> How do the slight touches of the chisel, the pencil, the pen, the fiddle-stick, etc.,—give the true swell, which gives the true pleasure!—O my countrymen! be nice!—be cautious of your language;—and never, O never let it be forgotten upon what small particles your eloquence and your fame depend.

It ought to be said that we who are the inheritors of the Bible and the great ritual of the Church, can hardly be worthy of our heritage unless our thoughts are clothed with the strong and austere speech of the Gospel. We all do well to realize that slovenly speech in ordinary conversation makes it that much more difficult to speak with dignity in the pulpit. We should be known as men who speak with a real love of words because we have learned that words carry within themselves the power to create and the power to destroy.

V

AS ONE HAVING
AUTHORITY

> "... the multitudes were as-
> tonished at his teaching: for
> he taught them ... not as
> their scribes."
>
> Matthew 7:28-29

There is probably no profession under fire so constantly
as the ministry. Every person feels that in this realm he is an
expert and can express his ideas as to what the preacher ought
to be doing that he is not doing, or why the preacher is doing
his job badly. The same person who feels some sense of humility when criticizing the medical or legal profession feels none
at all when attacking clergymen. Our generation has the
naïve idea that in the field of religion every man is a competent critic.

Most preachers learn to take this in their stride without
being too much bothered by it, although they are forced to
listen to much nonsense from ignorant people. On the whole,
it is a good thing for the pew to be free in its criticism of the
pulpit, and even in the good old days this was true. There
was a time when the preacher had more authority than he
has today simply because he was a preacher, but he never
lived in a tower and he has always been subject to criticism.

Yet I venture to suggest that there has been a change in the
general climate of pulpit criticism. There was a time when
the attack was made with vigor because men were deeply
concerned with religion. Great criticism is possible only when
its subject makes a difference. The sturdy Protestants of an
earlier day were often theologically cantankerous because

they were dealing with matters of life and death. One still finds that same spirit in some of the smaller, more intolerant sects. It is not something to defend or emulate, but it does reveal a serious attitude toward the preacher and his message.

Contemporary criticism is something else. So much of it is trivial and mere excuse hunting by men who would justify their Sunday golf or picnic. They treat the pulpit with an offhand superiority as if it were worth no more than a cheap compliment or a tolerant contempt. The preacher is not a voice from God, but a voice from a pious institution that for some vague reason or other it is best to let remain. If the preacher is fairly interesting, does not preach past twelve o'clock, and is a good mixer, he is to be tolerated. But if he is dull, long-winded, overly sanctimonious, or, worst of all, a radical, then he is to be removed as quickly as possible. The preacher is a sort of appendage, as when he is allowed to pronounce the benediction after a secular organization has conducted the service for a departed brother.

With certain notable exceptions, the ministry seems to have lost its authority. The great preacher, by the sheer force of his message and his personality, demands and receives respect for himself and his office, but the ministry in general has lost its power to exact the respect which is its due. In some ways this is strange, for in several particulars modern sermons are better than those of another day. There is more awareness of contemporary thought movements and a familiarity with science and economics. There are more illustrations and a greater effort to be practical. Yet, through it all, preaching has not been reborn and there is a general lack of confidence in the preaching process on the part of both laymen and ministers. There is often a desperate, sometimes pathetic attempt to revive the urgency and the significance of our function.

Perhaps the main cause of this is our enslavement in a naturalistic interpretation of our faith. With our uniqueness taken from us, we are at best only commentators on a process that will be neither hindered nor helped by our speaking. The poet may encourage the sea to break, or the river to flow on, but his word has no urgency for my own poor life. Neither has the preacher a word who does not come with a meaning beyond nature. Matthew Arnold's poem, subtitled significantly "To a Preacher," speaks to our condition:

> "In harmony with Nature?" Restless fool,
>   Who with such heat doth preach what were to thee,
>   When true, the last impossibility—
>   To be like Nature strong, like Nature cool!
>
> Know, man hath all which Nature hath, but more,
>   And in that *more* lie all his hopes of good.
>   Nature is cruel, man is sick of blood;
>   Nature is stubborn, man would fain adore;
>
> Nature is fickle, man hath need of rest;
>   Nature forgives no debt and fears no grave;
>   Man would be mild, and with safe conscience blest.
>
> Man must begin, know this, where Nature ends;
>   Nature and man can never be fast friends.
>   Fool, if thou canst not pass her, rest her slave!

We can be sure that we have little if any authority if we speak not for One who is more than nature. The church janitor who asked his minister one Sunday morning if he had any late news from God was expressing the longing in the hearts of men. Always the authority of the preacher goes back to a "thus saith the Lord." We are interpreters of a Voice that speaks, and not mere commentators on those generalities which we call the laws of nature.

Authority of Work

An American scholar, when asked if he was a D.D., replied, "Am I a D.D.? No, sir: I am not. Why, they give that wretched degree for preaching." The scorn in the heart of this man is not always expressed in words, but there is often a feeling that the preacher has one of the least demanding of jobs. The sermon is regarded as a conglomeration of little poems of inspiration, sweeping generalities in favor of virtuous action, and harmless, well-meaning advice which no practical person takes very seriously. Too many preachers allow this impression to go abroad because they are lazy men and their work is inept.

To put this matter of authority on its lowest plane, let us confess that too many preachers are content with second-rate performances. There is no time clock in the church and no prearranged schedule for a man to follow. He must be his own master, and only his conscience can give him guidance in the amount of work he does or the number of hours he puts into his task. It is a sad truth that many men in the ministry do not call very much, do not read very much, and could never hold a job where a reasonable amount of efficiency was demanded. All of this is apparent when they preach, and it is absurd to think that such as these can carry any authority for men who in their own businesses know the meaning of long and hard endeavor.

The artist is always a worker. We still marvel at the amount of work turned out by men like Rembrandt, or Rubens, or Stradivarius. It is not only a matter of brains and ability; there is the matter of the sheer physical part of it. Or there are the great churchmen like John Wesley. Did these men ever take time off for recreation? Had they never heard of nervous breakdowns? Were they never tired? Apparently not, for their output was terrific and their art seemed to release springs of power not available to more careful men.

None of us can rise higher than our own ideals of our profession, and the soft, pampered existence of some of us is forever a barrier between where we are now and the chance of growth in the ministry. Sometimes the greatest punishment God gives to a man is ease. There is a kind of authority that comes to any man who stands in his community as one who arises with the sun and is not afraid of burning a little midnight oil now and again. One of my friends once told me that when he was being questioned rather severely by his board for a position he had taken, he was helped greatly by the man who said, "However we may feel about this matter, we know that you are the hardest-working minister this church has ever had." Until a man has been saved from the idea that anything can be a substitute for just plain hard work, he may speak in a pleasant manner but he will never speak with authority.

With characteristic forthrightness George Bernard Shaw wrote:

> The artist who accounts for my personal disparagement by alleging personal animosity on my part is quite right. When people do less than their best, and do that at once badly and self-complacently, I hate them, I loathe them, detest them, long to tear them limb from limb and strew them in gobbets about the stage or platform. . . . The true critic is the man who becomes your personal enemy on the sole provocation of a bad performance, and will only be appeased by a good one.

The preacher needs to be as severe as that in regard to his own work.

The ministry is a full-time job from the moment one goes to his small rural church of forty members to the time when by the grace of God he may be called to the great cathedral with thousands of members and a large staff. There never was a church that did not demand more time than a man had to give it, or deserve more complete devotion than the best of us could muster. I never saw a man concerned with side issues who was worth his salt in the ministry. This is not to say that there are not many activities that the preacher will be called to carry on outside of his pulpit. But woe to the man who does not always remember that every activity he allows to claim his

time must be in the direction of helping him to better proclaim the Good News. A boy who joined the army, when
asked what his profession was, what his hobby was, what his
recreation was, replied to all these questions with one word:
"Poetry." And the preacher who is not able to be completely
absorbed in his job will lack one of the fundamental requirements for speaking with authority. Called to a task that has
no clear lines of limitation, we must learn how to leave many
intriguing side issues alone.

When John Livingston, a seventeenth-century English
preacher, spent the night in prayer and the early morning in
meditation, he preached a sermon that converted some five
hundred people. His only remark was that he got good assist-
ance upon the points he had meditated on. I should think so.
When Andrew Fuller was invited to a larger parish, he meditated on the matter for two years before he would leave his
little church of forty members. He it was who had said, "The
pulpit is an awful place, we preach for eternity." Men such
as these would certainly have something in their preaching
that the casual preacher does not have, and in fact, cannot
have.

A good many minutes are invested in an hour of worship.
There are enough places where people are invited to kill time
or spend it foolishly. The church where men cannot feel that
every unforgiving minute has sixty seconds worth of eternal
value has no right to complain if its pews are empty. That
throws a serious responsibility upon the preacher. He must
give forth his best judgment based on wide reading, careful
study, and long hours of preparation. He should be able to
say: "Here is my very best, and you may attend this service
and every service knowing that it will always be my very
best." It will not be possible to always "mount up with wings
as eagles," but it is always possible to do the hard work
faithfully.

John Haynes Holmes wrote in an article partly autobiographical:

> Now, when my work is all but done, and I have left only a
> few scant years of waning energy, I dream, as Charles Lamb
> dreamed of his children that were never born, of the sermons
> I might have preached, of the hymns I might have written, of
> the books I might have published, had I not given the best
> strength of my life to social causes. It is a real question—
> Was I wise or foolish in doing what I did? [1]

The growing sense of the importance of preaching in this
outstanding leader of liberal Christianity is most significant.
Dr. Holmes's contribution to the American Church has been
unique and I for one would not want him to have chosen any
different road. For us all, however, his testimony has weight,
when we consider our responsibility in bringing the Word
through preaching, and bringing it with authority.

This is as good a place as any to consider the matter of
manuscript versus notes versus neither. The answer to me is
clear: The way to preach is without manuscripts or notes, for
there is added effectiveness, not to say authority, to the
preacher who can speak directly to men. There are those who
can write their sermons and read them with ease and grace.
There are other men who use outlines or sketchy notes without letting them be too prominent. All of this is true, but
other things being equal, the man who stands without written support finds his way to the wills of his hearers with more
directness and welcome than any of the others. For those of
us who have been using one method or the other for many
years, it is perhaps too late to make it worth while learning a
new way. But for every young man who is beginning his ministry, let it be said that no other method but the extemporaneous one should be considered. It is worth all it costs, and
many a fine preacher has surrendered a large percentage of
his power to manuscripts and notes.

---

[1] *Christian Century Pulpit*, December, 1945.

It is sometimes objected that one man has a memory and another has none. That simply is not true, and any man can learn to stand on his feet and preach with freedom. For it is largely a matter of habit, and if the sermon is organized logically, and if a preacher goes over it a few times during the week, he will soon learn to be proficient in this manner of delivery. I remember arriving at a student church one Sunday morning with my notes thirty miles away in my room. That desperate moment was my conversion and it was one of the best things that ever happened to me.

We are speakers, not writers; we are preachers, not lecturers. It would be quite futile and wholly undesirable to seek a proof-text for this or any other method of preaching. But if preaching is the bringing of truth through personality, it will carry the most weight when it flows most freely from the preacher to the congregation. Let a man be thoroughly prepared, and let the message come with a spontaneity as if God at that particular moment were directly addressing the will of each man. Such delivery carries an authority with it that is like a simple call to arms. Written stuff is like so many crutches for a limping message to lean on.

Preacher as Expert

In our time the expert has been in bad repute, for there have been too many politicians pretending to have knowledge they never had. Men skilled in one field have assumed the prerogative of speaking in every other field. Sooner or later it begins to dawn upon us that the world's champion heavyweight boxer may not necessarily know how to control inflation, nor the military mind be a trustworthy guide into the future. Since the preacher is supposed to know only about spiritual things anyway, which means to most men impractical things, his pronouncements are often looked upon with suspicion if not with downright contempt. Because the field is so wide, the preacher's more general knowledge is often

defined as knowing nothing about everything. In contrast to
the scientist, who knows "facts" about a definable field, the
preacher is regarded with disdain and contempt when he
deals with "values" which refuse to be seen under the
microscope.

It was not always so. The preacher was one time called
"the man of God," and his knowledge of the road to heaven
was respected. Only when he serves an institution that claims
to have a monopoly on the knowledge of how to be saved can
he expect to have that kind of authority today. Yet the
preacher is every man's superior in religion, or ought to be,
and he meets men on his own ground every Sunday when
he preaches. We need not expect, nor do most of us desire, a
kind of blind subservience to our office, but we should give
the impression of knowledge and experience in the places
where men are confronted by God in Christ. It is the sort of
respect that is given only when it is earned and deserved,
which is the only real respect there is anyway.

This lack of command in the pulpit is rather generally
recognized, but the solution is often wrong. A man some
time ago dreamed of the church of the future and saw it
under the direction of a preacher who would consult experts
in other fields before he ventured an opinion in those fields.
Thus he would have available a board who would give him
the authoritative information about economics, or international relations, or political science. It should be said that
this was not a dream but a nightmare. What expert would
you put on the board, and which one would you believe when
they disagreed? For the truth of the matter is that men in
these fields differ as markedly as theologians. But more serious than this criticism is the total lack of comprehension as
to what kind of expert the preacher ought to be.

It is not because we do not know enough about science,
or politics, or manufacturing problems, that we are lacking
in authority. I know men who are experts in particular

fields of social life, and still they do not speak with convicting power. The pulpit is as accurate and informed in these matters as most platforms in the world, but our lost power is not restored. This is not to counsel carelessness in this realm of our preaching, nor is it to suggest that inaccuracies are to be tolerated. But it is to say that the sign of the expert in the pulpit does not lie there.

It does not lie in the realm of business administration either. Some churches have decided that they need such men to direct their great plants and their far-flung program, and so they do. No man can despise these matters and do justice to his calling. But such churches and such men have their reward, for they have not heard a prophetic voice, nor seen a vision, nor dreamed a dream in years. This kind of pulpit carries remarkably little weight, for the congregation is surrounded by that kind of atmosphere all week.

What men want in the pulpit is a man like David Dickson, the seventeenth-century Scotch preacher. A merchant said of him: "That man showed me all my heart." This is the place where the preacher ought to be an expert. It is perhaps noteworthy that John Wesley's effective ministry did not begin until that night in the Aldersgate Chapel when he "felt his heart strangely warmed." When we become experts in interpreting how the grace of God finds its way into the heart of a sinner, then we shall speak with a note of command, and our people will listen in a new way. The expert may at times be merely a man far from home, but if he is real, he is a man who has been to the place he describes, and able to tell how a thing ought to be done because he has done it himself. Remember how St. Francis in his *Little Flowers* refers to "the example of Christ, who began to do before he began to teach."

There are many things we do not know and many fields in which we are not at home. But as the Book of Hebrews says, while we do not see all things subjected unto him yet, we do see Jesus. In that vision there is the clue to the spiritual problems of men. If we endeavor to adapt the Gospel to our own or any social system, we shall have no clear word to speak. But if we are concerned only with what the spirit of Christ demands in the face of a particular need, then we shall speak with directness and authority.

A teacher of history told his class that they could pick up their facts out of books, but that in his class they could expect only their interpretation. It is in the Christian interpretation and criticism of life that we are expected to be experts. What do all the facts mean? Because we have an answer that is unique, we can restore the lost glory to the pulpit. We shall begin to do that when we realize that our proclamation is of a special Act, and that we are called to speak out of our own special knowledge to people who often know very little about it.

It is time that a good many preachers awaken to the disturbing fact that much of Christianity is unknown territory to a fearfully large number of people. The ignorance of churchmen concerning some of the fundamentals of our faith is alarming, and when one begins to talk to those outside the Church, he is overwhelmed. How can one speak a message to men who do not even know how to ask the right questions? Where does one begin in proclaiming the Gospel when the most elementary terms are foreign to his listeners?

The answer seems to be that we must do as missionaries do or as the first-century Christians did. We must define the Gospel. We will be wrong if we assume that our congregations are familiar with the meaning of our great doctrines. If this is distressing, it is also a restoration of our status as experts in a field of the utmost importance. No longer do we need to be concerned about speaking of things familiar to our people. The old, old story has a freshness about it today that will give to the man who tells it with clearness a new authority.

Experience

In C. H. Spurgeon's *My Sermon Notes*, published in 1888, he said, "I am more than ever impressed with the conviction that men must not only preach that which they have themselves thought over, and prepared, but also that which they have themselves experienced in its life and power." Yet every interpretation of Christianity which makes it primarily an inner experience needs to be on its guard lest it transform our religion into something too subjective. It is not impossible for doctors to treat diseases they have never had. We could not live one day without accepting and using things we have never experienced and do not understand. Many of us would want to ask a good many questions of any person who would confine our preaching to that which we have experienced.

Yet the differences between these two points of view are probably due more to definition than to ultimate disagreement. There are vast truths which we believe and preach, though in a sense we have never experienced and never can experience them. The young man beginning his ministry will preach a shallow and limited gospel if he confines himself only to what he has actually experienced. So will the man of seventy-five. We are always going beyond our own experiences and we are always leaning heavily on the testimony of the saints. The Gospel is too big and too profound for any man to say that he has experienced it in its completeness. The glory of the Great Tradition is that we are a part of something beyond us and we are speakers for great mysteries which stretch out before us like the ocean while we stand on the shore.

Yet the man who dares to speak words which are only words to him will be little better than the man who hires a ghost writer to prepare his speeches. The word has to pass through the processes of our own thinking, and the mystery has to be caught in the web of our own personality. The truth must strike a responsive note in our hearts before it belongs to us. If faith means anything, it means that we can go beyond our actual experience and yet have an assurance that we have not gone astray. I think the final criterion of whether or not something beyond our experience really belongs to us is whether or not our hearts say "yes."

I had a great teacher one time who troubled me more than any man I ever met. He spoke with assurance about Christian ideas which I had never experienced and which represented an orthodoxy I had been warned against. Yet the words fell with mighty impact upon my mind and, in spite of my increasingly feeble attempts to deny, they would not be dismissed. I think the thing that made it so difficult to escape was the certainty that he was speaking easily and with assurance of something that was as real to him as breathing. I believe he influenced me more than any single person I ever knew because the authority of his experience was too great to be denied.

The Gospel does not find each man in precisely the same way. We are all different and we are all predestined to interpret our faith from a point of view different from that of any other man. The beginning preacher has not yet found this experience, as a rule. Sometimes it takes several years before a preacher discovers what the essential nature of the Gospel is to him. It may come upon him gradually, or it may come in sudden dramatic fashion as it did to Horace Bushnell, who leaped out of bed one night and cried: "I have found it. I have found the Gospel." What he meant was that his own life and mind had suddenly been illuminated with a vision of what the Gospel was to him. This does not mean a departure from the orthodox tradition but rather the normative experience from which all of a man's preaching will be fed. And it is the birth of an assurance and confidence that the preacher never had before, and without which he never preaches with authority.

There is no substitute for experience; the wider a man's life has ranged, the more certainty there is in his message. The sheltered life is not for the preacher, and he should not strive to live in a study. Such men will hear the voice of their Lord when it is too late, calling them out from their safe place into the suffering world. Remember Brewer Mattocks' parish priest who, when called from the steeple to die, asked the Master where he was. And the answer came back, "Down here among my people!" To travel widely, to know many different kinds of people, to be at home with all classes and conditions of men gives the preacher's message compulsion.

Yet we would be wrong if we assumed that only by actually going through an experience can we know enough about it to help another man endure it. God has given us imagination so that we may weep with those who weep and laugh with those who laugh. This is more important than much running about. Great literature will lead us into the inner experiences of men if we read with imagination, but just bulk in our reading will fail to widen our experience. In a sense no experience can give us anything more than we have brought to it. But having achieved that inner sensitiveness, there is hardly a happening so trivial that it does not add a note of personal urgency to our preaching.

There is a kind of preacher who has a very intelligent and adequate theology but who never moves men to believe it and be saved through their believing it. There is also the kind of preacher without education or adequate training for his task who converts men by the sheer power of his own assurance. Something has happened to him, and even cultured people know that he is proclaiming a way of life that he knows about and believes in with all his heart. From such humble presentations men are more often led to the realization of their own dreams than from a more intellectual presentation of something that obviously has not been deeply experienced. Wisely does St. Paul say that experience worketh hope, which means for the preacher that cynical men can hope again if they catch the note of authority from his message which must rest on his experience.

The Scriptures and Other Books

A preacher remarked to me that he wished he knew the Bible as well as his father had known it. Yet this man had been to seminary and studied both Greek and Hebrew. Still he did not know his English Bible as well as a man who had never been to college but had simply read because he loved it. Many of us would have to confess the same thing if we awakened to the fact that we have been reading books about the Bible but have not spent much time in reading the Book itself. I am impressed with the added authority that comes to the man who is at home in the Bible and can bring the great passages into his sermon with ease. This can release a simple discourse from triteness, and it restores beauty and drama to our preaching.

We have been through a critical and destructive period in the study of the Bible. It has been a time of controversy and bitter feeling in some quarters. Those who were enamored of certain theories of Biblical criticism often attacked their adversaries with a brutal disregard for the sacred and holy places in their lives. On the other hand, men on the defensive sometimes shut their minds to truth and light in a vain attempt to protect what seemed to them an inviolable holy of holies. Men are never at their best when they are on the defensive, and those who are attacking hardly ever maintain the necessary objectivity demanded by truth.

For the most part, the controversy is now ended and Biblical criticism has won its right to recognition. Most of us will not have to pay much heed to heresy hunters or to self-appointed champions of the inerrancy of the Bible. The controversy has had mostly good results, for the Bible is a much greater and more useful book for having been subject to the attacks of enemies and the defense of friends. No man who has passed from the position of the extreme Biblical literalist to that of the man who now accepts the main conclusions of the higher criticism can doubt but that the Book has gained much.

The time has now arrived for preachers to realize that the destructive part of the criticism was just clearing away so much dead brush. Now we are in a position to use the Bible and preach the Bible more effectively than either our narrow fundamentalists or our radical modernists. We may have settled the question of who wrote a particular book, when he wrote it, and what essentially he was endeavoring to communicate. But we still have left unanswered the most important question of all, namely: Is it true, and if so, what is its implication for me now? It is time for preaching to be concerned primarily with the latter questions.

Ours is not a religion based on a book, it is true, for the center of Christianity is the personality of Jesus. But the Bible is the great textbook of the spiritual meaning of life and the story of God's search for men and His way of dealing with us. In every hour of crisis, the Bible speaks with increasing authority and guidance. One of the most dangerous characteristics of our generation is that it knows so little about the Bible and might almost be called a generation of Bible illiterates.

Modern preaching needs the authority of the Bible in it, and we can do nothing better than to return to Biblical preaching. This is not to say that we should return to use of the Scriptural phrases and a telling of Biblical stories as ends in themselves. May we be delivered from proof-text preaching! But the modern preacher whose roots go deep into the Bible will discover a new element in his message that carries with it an element of claim. If a man can carry his congregation into a new and deeper understanding of the Scriptures, he has done them a very great service. We need to bring our people into the atmosphere of this Book which, in a deeper sense than we realized, is the Word of God. For it is here that we see the meaning of history, the patience of God as He works out His long purposes, and the miracle of the Incarnation.

There is much to be said in favor of textual preaching. No one would want to insist that every sermon must have a text, but the preacher who has departed from texts entirely is missing much. A great text keeps us in line with the Christian tradition and often contains insights that enrich our whole interpretation of the Gospel. It is a sharp and terse summing up of the sermon's thought and is more easily remembered by the congregation. How often we read a verse in the Bible and there comes back to us a noble sermon preached on it.

Yet there are dangers associated with textual preaching. In Yorick's sermon notes in *Tristram Shandy*, Sterne writes of a certain text: "The excellency of this text is, that it will suit any sermon—and of this sermon—that it will suit any text." It hardly needs to be said that if we use the Bible in this way, it weakens instead of strengthens our preaching. There is a kind of preacher who in the name of treating a text exhaustively in reality puts into it all that his own silly mind can think about. If there was a revolt against preaching from texts, it was due to this habit of men's using texts as convenient pegs to hang their own thoughts on.

If we believe that it is legitimate to make of the Bible a wax nose, as one critic of the allegorical method put it, that is one thing of course. Nothing can be said to such a person for he begins with a premise that makes it impossible for our minds to meet. But if we can agree that there is an integrity in the Scriptures which any honest man must respect, then we must be on our guard lest we go too far in our attempt to show "how much there is in a verse." Sometimes we can appear to be very clever in our misuse of Scripture, but it is a cheap reward unworthy of any serious preacher. Believe me, not every chance idea that comes into my head as I look at a verse was put there by divine inspiration.

Truly the Bible must speak its own word and not ours. We have a perfect right to be free in our speaking, but if we want to have our message undergirded with the Great Book, then we must not twist or modify it. We shall discover that there is no need for such manipulation. No generation of preachers had the knowledge or the information available, as we have it, to make the Bible the most interesting book as well as the most helpful book in the world. It is too bad that just at the time when these new and marvelous discoveries are available, people in general should be so unconcerned about the Bible. We can, therefore, bring a new authority into our preaching by rooting it deeply in the Scriptures and thus bringing their drama and truth to ears that have not heard before. A great deal of American preaching in the long armistice between the two world wars was passed by lightly because it did not go back any farther than last year's book or this morning's newspaper.

We must have the scholar's temperament and habit or we will be drained dry in a year. Much of our reading will not contribute directly to our sermons, but it will be there by implication. The well-read preacher reveals by a word here or a reference there that he is aware of the thought currents of his day and has taken the trouble to learn the theories of his time. Such a man will not be driven to fall back upon the last book he managed to read, and fill his sermon with it to the distress of the better-read people of his congregation. Nor will a single book become too important.

Mortimer Adler has pointed out that books fall into two main categories: (1) digests and repetitions, and (2) original communications. That is, the vast number of books published are simply restatements of what has been said before. But there are a number of books, often termed "the classics," which are foundations of civilization. These are the ones a man needs to know, and it is relatively unimportant whether or not he has read the last "best seller." Clifton Fadiman says that while he has read five or ten thousand books in the last two decades, he probably would be a wiser man if he had read only fifteen, and they the right ones.

However, I am convinced that a preacher must be aware of contemporary literature if for no other reason than to know what kind of literary fodder is being consumed. When it comes to the proportion of time one should spend on particular types of reading, that must be left to one's own judgment. Rules are fine, but the busy preacher will soon discover that he must grasp a minute here and a half-hour there. Some books are to be read in a hurry, but only a fool will try to skim a book like Toynbee's *Study of History*. Yet the preacher who wants to speak with authority must learn to read rapidly and with discrimination.

Exaggeration

We are men who deal with the intangibles and the affairs of the unseen. If we are to be effective preachers, we must have imagination, enthusiasm, sensitivity, and faith. Like everything else, these gifts carry with them great temptations to become careless in their use. The scientist must learn to sit at the feet of facts like a little child, to use Huxley's phrase, and he can be checked if he is not thoroughly honest in his statements. The preacher is confined to no such definite limits and is free to speak about the big things which eye hath not seen nor ear heard.

As a result, preachers often fall into the habit of exaggeration. They do not mean to be dishonest, but they have never severely disciplined themselves to speak with extreme care and restraint. Under the excitement of the actual delivery of the sermon, we tend to speak of "the greatest," "the best," "the worst." Often such statements will not stand close scrutiny, and in our own cooler moments we would be the first to see that we overstated the proposition.

Or we tend to overemphasize one truth in order to make our point and pass swiftly over a fact that would weaken our homiletic interpretation. This is not done deliberately as a rule, but it is a vicious habit which becomes worse with the years. The time comes when a careful thinker and scholar dismisses our preaching with contempt for he spots the distortions of our message. Like the boy who cried "Wolf" too often, we may become those whom no one believes until he has carefully investigated for himself.

This is one reason why so much preaching carries with it little authority. It becomes unnecessarily repulsive, as Channing said of the preaching of Theodore Parker, who was guilty of dealing too much in exaggerations. A reviewer of some of G. K. Chesterton's essays wrote: "Paradox ought to be used like onions to season a salad. Mr. Chesterton's salad is all onions. Paradox has been defined as 'Truth standing on her head to attract attention.' Mr. Chesterton makes Truth cut her throat to attract attention." So a man may do the same thing with exaggerations.

Wherever it is possible, a preacher should be as exact in his statements as a professor or a scientist. If we are not sure about a statement, we ought to make it clear that we are not sure. Facts are stubborn things and can wreck our influence if we deal with them carelessly. Even as the preacher should expect no special treatment in his community, so should he be as responsible for his statements as the most careful thinker. Hardly anything so weakens our position as overstatement, and preachers would do well to learn the effectiveness of understatement. When God called me to the ministry He did not give me the right to deal with truth as if it existed to suit my own convenience. We will do much toward restoring the lost authority to the pulpit if we begin to develop a more sensitive conscience toward the precise use of words.

VI

AFTER I HAVE PREACHED TO OTHERS

". . . lest by any means . . .
I myself should be rejected."
I Corinthians 9:27

One of the most disturbing things to the preacher is the assumption on the part of the laity that he is above temptation and sin. In spite of an era which expects the minister to play the part of the "regular fellow" in the service of a God who is described as an easygoing grandfather, there is still the feeling that preachers live a sheltered life quite safe from lusts of the flesh and the more refined evils of the spirit. More than once a parishioner has intimated that he wished he could find faith as easily as it must be for me. But there is a sense in which the minister is the most tempted of men and only an extra portion of the grace of God can keep him from being the worst of sinners. One of my friends said in an address to ministers that there would be preachers in hell. That was taken up as an extreme statement by the press, but it seems a perfectly commonplace remark to any man who is still sensitive to the pitfalls of the ministry. "Everybody talkin' 'bout heav'n ain't goin' there."

Pride

If any man doubts our special danger in this matter of pride, let him read again his Bible. Usually a great obstacle in the way of God's will for Israel was the priestly caste which preferred a place of honor in the *status quo* to the rule of justice in society. It is true that we may consider ourselves in the line of the prophets and heir to their tradition, but let us remember that as a rule they were not a professional class. Jesus was not nearly so denunciatory of publicans and harlots as he was of the pious and their spokesmen. We are of all men most open to what Christianity regards as the fundamental sin, namely, pride.

It should not be forgotten that many of the great spokesmen for God were laymen. That is true because the professional religious leader tends to become too proud to sit at the feet of Jesus in humility. Most of us have laymen in our churches who put us to shame by the simple, beautiful, Christlike lives they live in comparison with our own sham-tinged existence.

We will all have criticism, some of it unfair and cruel, but we will have also more flattery than most men can endure without having their heads turned. Too often we stand at the center of the stage, and too much we must be in the public eye and the recipients of the public's applause. We are well-known figures in our communities and we receive extra services and special politenesses beyond our just deserving. It is too easy to come to the place where we assume that adulation is our due. The popular preacher is in even greater danger than the popular actor. Perhaps this is what Charles Wesley had in mind when he wrote in his *Journal:* "I marvel that any preacher should be saved."

Preachers, like teachers, often enjoy having disciples who look upon them as the master. Too many times a little coterie of the past preacher's disciples are the thorn in the flesh of the new preacher and stand in the way of the onward march of the church. We had better react as Walter Pater did when an undergraduate served him his tea kneeling. Pater muttered: "Get up, you fool." Sentimental homage cannot always be prevented but it need never be encouraged.

This pride, which is the most unlovely of characteristics, becomes especially apparent at ministerial conferences. A man asks a question or makes a remark, not to contribute anything to the matter at hand or to gain information, but to show how important he is and what a fine job he is doing in his church. How cleverly the fact that many members were taken in last year, or a budget of many thousands of dollars was increased, or the preacher is a clever and important person is dragged into the remarks. The truth is that many a preacher rivals Hollywood when it comes to a shameless kind of exhibitionism. How pleasant it is to find a great preacher who is at the same time a humble man, and the fact that we do find him makes it plain that preachers can find salvation from their besetting sin of pride.

Some years ago when I was a student, I was asked to interview several of the outstanding preachers in the West concerning their Sunday evening programs, as the basis of a paper I was writing. I can remember yet those who took the opportunity to inform me what important men they were and how presumptuous I was to intrude upon their time. But the greatest of them all made me feel so much at home and so welcome that it still lifts up my heart when I think of him. It is a sad day for any one of us when people who would speak to us, whether they are young or old, rich or poor, feel some doubt as to whether we can forget ourselves long enough to be sincerely interested in them. Verily, such as these have their reward.

Our only safety is to keep always under the spirit of the One who for our sakes became poor. If our periods of self-satisfaction are not counterbalanced, then it is only a matter of time until we begin to take ourselves more seriously than we should. If the habit of prayer remains with us, there is hope that the veneer of pride which covers us all can be cracked and the spirit of God can do its healing work. No man who is being informed constantly of how much good he is doing and what a good man he is can remain humble by himself. But if we ask God constantly to make us realize that we are unprofitable servants, perhaps then we can keep from thinking of ourselves more highly than we ought to think.

The preacher needs a good sense of humor for many reasons, but there is no place where it can function more advantageously than in this matter of pride. Sometimes our only safety is to see ourselves and our pretensions as laughable. The *stuffed shirt* is a man who is afraid to laugh at himself because it would puncture his blown-up importance, and so he is afraid to laugh at anything. If we can keep sensitive to the sheer joy of the Lord and remember that important phrase in the Old Testament, "God laughed," we will not be able to maintain the false sense of our own importance. There is sometimes a pride which not even prayer can remove, but it will go out with well-aimed humor. Perhaps it was this that made one of our leading theologians say in all seriousness that it was more important for a preacher to have a certain humor magazine on his shelves than the latest book about theology. The point is that pride is such a serious temptation to us that we must be prepared to take heroic precautions against it.

Cervantes said, "He preaches well who lives well." The proud preacher is not willing to preach through a Christlike living, but must always be heading a committee or finding a prominent place in a crusade. It is still true that when God called us to be His ministers, He called us to walk humbly with Him. The preacher who preaches to himself as well as to his congregation will be more likely to keep his pride under control than the one who believes that preaching is entirely a one-way passage. Dean Willard L. Sperry as a young assistant once reproved an elderly colleague thus: "Here in this city where everybody is busy making and selling cotton cloth, I can't see the use to these people of your yearly sermon on astronomy." "My boy," replied the old veteran, "of course it is of no use at all, but it greatly enlarges my idea of God."

And perhaps the best way to keep our own smallness apparent to ourselves is to consciously seek to enlarge our ideas of the One we serve.

Becoming Professionalized

One of the most devastating and penetrating criticisms of preachers who become merely professional word-users is in Kierkegaard's *For Self-Examination, etc.* He points out how prone we are to make sure of our own security and then to preach daring to other men. What right have we to counsel courage to others unless we have risked something for the Gospel in our own careers? We talk about Christianity as a possibility or as something that once happened in the past, but we shrink from facing the implications of our faith as a present demand and as a present possibility. We get all the rank and the decorations possible, but then we preach a Gospel which despises such things. We see ourselves as promoters of a product which serves our own need for a profession. Kierkegaard writes:

> Not inversely, as Christianity was preached in a later age, that it is the physician who "needs the patients," the teacher who needs the pupils, and therefore, as a matter of course (like any other salesman, who surely does not require that the highly esteemed public should buy a pig in a poke), must be at your service with reasons, proofs, recommendations from others who have been cured or instructed, etc.[1]

What this man sees so clearly is our tendency to become just a profession with an eye on the main chance and personal aggrandizement.

Nowhere do we need the grace of God more than when we are dealing with money. The laborer is worthy of his hire and the preacher does his church no favor if he allows it to underpay him. As long as we operate under a system in which the

---

[1] Kierkegaard, *For Self-Examination and Judge For Yourselves,* Princeton, 1944, chapter on "Becoming Sober."

preacher's status is judged by his salary, a man has a right to a salary commensurate with his ability and in proportion to the total budget of the church he serves. John Wesley's advice is still to the point when he urges Christians to earn all they can without hurting their Christian conscience or their neighbors; to save all they can and not spend to gratify pride or the ego; and then to give all they can. Preachers who rightly interpret the spirit of these rules will have guidance for their finances.

Yet no man should forget the temptation that he stands under constantly, to make money more important than it ought to be. Let none of us be so naïve as to think that, since we have entered a profession which is not noted for large financial rewards, we are therefore released from all further concern with greed. This not only is a temptation to the city pastor of the large church, but affects the small-salaried man as well. There is hardly anything more injurious to our work than the impression that we are interested primarily in money. A great deal of the ill repute of some mass evangelism campaigns was due to the feeling on the part of many laymen that they had become financial rackets. Too much money was taken from the community by methods that fitted the huckster better than they did the prophet of God.

The preacher will do well to lean over backwards in handling his financial affairs with openness and honesty. Let him not think that there is any reason for abusing his credit, and if there is not a determination to pay for what he gets, then he must do without it. This is no place for self-pity to take control of us and whisper that we are not as other men. It may be granted that we serve our brethren for small salaries, but it does not follow that the ordinary ethics of buying and selling do not apply to us. Whether we make one thousand dollars a year or ten thousand, we must live within our income. Hardly anything so destroys the dignity of the ministry as a preacher who does not pay his bills.

Much bitterness and wrangling can be eliminated if the preacher has his financial arrangements with his church clearly stated. One of my friends told me when I was being interviewed by a church committee to be sure and state clearly what I expected in the way of salary, moving expenses, etc. "For," said he, "there is almost sure to be trouble if that is not decided upon. But once it has been discussed frankly, then it can be set aside and forgotten." I think that is good advice. The church loses its respect for a man who seems to be expecting more than the church feels it is under obligation to provide. Something has been accomplished if the church and the minister can provide the community with an object lesson in how Christians ought to handle their business and financial affairs.

Nor should the preacher consider himself excused from bearing his share of the financial program of the church. It is all nonsense to talk about our ability to earn so much more in some other work that we are excused from giving to the Christian program. For one thing we do not know how we would have done in other work, and in the second place, such talk is a denial of the majesty of our calling. We are stewards as all our laymen are, and any man who whines about the sacrifices he has made for the ministry ought to be ashamed of himself. In the percentage of my income which I give to the building of the Kingdom, I ought to be an example to my laymen.

To deal with sacred matters and remain sincere in handling them is a task beyond our strength unless we are upheld by the One to whom all of life was sacred. Our insincerity is not always a conscious thing, but it creeps in upon us unexpectedly. In our intimate services at the time of death, how easily we become callous to the heartbreak of people, and see them as just another funeral situation. That we have to become somewhat hardened as a matter of simple survival is true. But the preacher can so easily be like the comforters of

Job, glib but unconvincing because we do not share each other's woes. These lines express it:

> The toad beneath the harrow knows
> Exactly where each tooth-point goes;
> The butterfly, upon the road,
> Preaches contentment to the toad.

We are dealers with the emotions of men and we cannot function properly without being skilled in appealing to the emotions. That means that we are often carried away beyond the bounds of our normal sensibility. There is no sin in this for we must sharpen the awareness of our people. But little by little there creeps in on us the over-emotionalized viewpoint, which means that we tend to despise plain truth and must always dress it up. The time comes when we can no longer distinguish between fact and interpretation so that our discourse lacks sincerity. Truth tends to be regarded as too blunt for our purposes.

An old New Hampshire farmer was listening to an over-glib, over-enthusiastic speaker and he remarked, "Wall, he talks consid'abul as I do when I'm lyin'." He caught the false note because he recognized it out of his own experience. That will be true of our listeners who know the temptation in their own lives and are quick to spot it in the preacher. Our speaking becomes too smooth and easy to stab the heart, and we become mere professional orators.

The professional preacher is not so interested in transforming the world as he is in transforming the Gospel to provide a fitting background for his own efforts. How easily the center of importance shifts with the passing years until all unconsciously we have usurped the center and Christ has become a means to our own end. If any man enters his pulpit not under the control of the spirit of worship, he may be sure that the center of the service will not be God but rather his own fine ability to define his own feelings about God. Let any man who has a conscience in this matter spend a few minutes alone after every service and ask himself: "Did I really worship God this morning?" For the disease is not sudden but gradual, and to keep unspotted by the slow stain of insincerity is a task demanding constant vigilance.

It is too easy to become satisfied with a competent, professional doing of our job. When Chalmers was first called to Kilmany, he taught mathematics and chemistry at St. Andrews, telling his father that Saturday was sufficient to give to the preparation of his sermons. But he changed his mind later when he discovered that there was more to it than speaking easily and gracefully. Nothing is worse done than that which is done merely professionally for religion. It is not only the evil that results, but the good which might have been accomplished and was not. For the shallow preaching that is striving primarily for effect and popularity is never able to blast the rocks of prejudice and sin.

Ezekiel has a good description of such a preacher:

> And they come unto thee as the people cometh, and they sit before thee as my people, and they hear thy words, but do them not; for with their mouth they show much love, but their heart goeth after their gain. And, lo, thou art unto them as a very lovely song of one that hath a pleasant voice, and can play well on an instrument; for they hear thy words, but they do them not.[2]

This kind of response is not always the preacher's fault, as Ezekiel makes clear. But there is a kind of preacher who finds his reward in this kind of listening and neither expects nor desires any other reaction to his words.

In his autobiography George Antheil, the composer, points out how music copyists, who are often disappointed composers, come to judge a music writer by the neatness of his score page. One of them bought himself a facsimile of a Beethoven symphony so that he could have before him the proof that

2 Ezekiel 33:31–32.

Beethoven did a slovenly job when it came to laying out a score.[3] The next best thing for the man who cannot create the music is to copy it neatly, but what a sad thing it is when the man has convinced himself that neat copying is better than rough creativeness. May God keep us from preferring neat shallowness to rugged depths.

One of the sure signs of the development of the professional viewpoint is the appearance of the artistic temperament. We begin to pamper ourselves and guide our work by way of our feelings. We are artists, and therefore we are not to be treated as ordinary mortals but should expect special favors and special considerations. An old minister growled out his contempt for this attitude in these words: "My dear fellow, of course I don't always *feel* like praying, and preaching when Sunday morning comes round, but that has nothing to do with the case. I have my work to do, and I do it as honestly and straightforwardly as I can, saying to God and man what ought to be said at that time." Preaching is an art, but there is no place in it for a spoiled, egocentric artist.

Preaching but Not Being

There is an old English play of the sixteenth century which gives the following instructions for costuming the characters: "Let idolatry be decked lyke an olde wytche, Sodomy lyke a monke of all sectes, Ambycyon lyke a byshop, Covetousness lyke a popysh doctour, and Hypocresy lyke a graye fryre." [4] After we have made due allowances for satire, we see a suspicion on the part of that generation that the Christian Gospel was not always incarnated in the lives of its servants. In every age the failure of the clergy to practice what they preach has been the subject of much criticism, some of it bitter and some of it sad. Milton said that the true poet ought himself to be a

---

[3] Antheil, *Bad Boy of Music,* Doubleday, Doran, 1945, 127.
[4] Cheney, *The Theatre,* Tudor, 1939.

true poem, and people feel that the true preacher ought himself to be a sermon.

The truth apparent to every man who is a clergyman is that speaking about a great thing does not necessarily give the power to exemplify it. In fact, there is a sense in which just the opposite is true, and precisely because we speak of these things continually, we find it that much more difficult to practice them. Carlyle wrote: "It is a sad but sure truth that every time you speak of a fine purpose, especially if with eloquence and to the admiration of bystanders, there is the less chance of your ever making a fact of it in your own poor life." Yet I suppose there is no part of our work so misunderstood as this. Most people assume that men who talk about Christianity constantly are automatically in a better position to practice it than others. But actually, it is as if much speaking blunts the edge of the word when it tries to penetrate the heart of the speaker.

Not many preachers would dare say with St. Paul, "For yourselves know how ye ought to imitate us." [5] How clever we become at going around this plain obligation. We talk about the necessity of reforming the church and changing society, but no man dares to face his personal responsibility to become an illustration of his message. It is a weakness of the ministry that it spends too much energy in delivery of the message and gives too little attention to the living of it.

Let us never believe that our duty is done when we have spoken well for the Gospel. Quintilian told his fellow citizens in Rome that "an orator is a good man speaking well," and Cato had the same thought: "An orator is a good man skilled in speaking." What these great pagans understood was that no man can separate his character from his speaking any more than he can separate his character from any undertaking. There is a sense in which even the truth becomes sullied

_____

5 II Thessalonians 3:7.

and unlovely when it comes out of hypocrisy. Bishop McDowell's words ought to be inscribed on the conscience of every
preacher: "For we never understand the cross until we endure
it or the atonement until we practice it." [6]

God's activity in finding persons through the preacher demands that the words shall have a clear channel. If the people
present in the congregation hear words and look into eyes
with the feeling that the sermon has not first of all permeated
the person of the preacher and found a welcome in his heart,
they can hardly find the power to appropriate it for their own
needs. For this there is no substitute, and when it is present,
it covers a multitude of weaknesses.

Critics of the theater point out how now and again an
amateur who feels his part and for the time seems to actually
be living it, will reach the heights which the professional actor
can attain only after a lifetime of training. There is an inner
quality for which external competency can never quite substitute. It is probably true also that the inspired amateur will
be even more effective after he has learned the skills of the
professional, if he does not lose his divine fire in the process.
Which is to say that the preacher no more than the actor can
divorce the inner experience from the techniques and be an
adequate instrument for the Word.

The history of the Christian Church has been made glorious by its great servants who, like Jesus, made a unity out of
their lives and their message. It was said that Bernard of
Clairvaux had so compelling a personality that when he came
to a village to speak, mothers hid their sons from him, wives
their husbands, and companions their friends. For there was
in him not only a word but the incarnation of the word.
George Herbert, the seventeenth-century English country
parson, was so beloved by his people "that they would let
their plough rest when Mr. Herbert's saint's-bell rung to

---

[6] McDowell, *Good Ministers of Jesus Christ*, Abingdon, 1917, 14.

prayers, that they might also offer their devotions to God with him, and would then return back to their plough." Men like these have made their messages saving powers and unforgettable experiences for by being what they were, they made every man better than he would have otherwise been.

We have our Elmer Gantrys in the ministry, as any man knows. But they are rare, and most of us are somewhere in between that kind of preacher on the one hand and a saint like George Herbert on the other. And when we are discouraged with our ministry and our own feeble attempts to be what we ought to be, we meet some great and humble soul within our fellowship, and we are encouraged to keep on trying. We stand now and again with the men who come from the small and difficult churches whose dress is plain and whose speech is rough. They never made more than fifteen hundred dollars in one year and out of that meager salary they have educated their children and maintained their homes. The purchase of a new book had to be planned for because the budget was already stretched to the breaking point. They have been through droughts and crop failures and have shared their neighbors' poverty without whimpering. Sometimes they are a little narrow in their views, but they are ever willing to go to battle for a conviction, for the dignity of man, and for the supremacy of conscience. In spite of all that they lack, their homes produce great men and women, future leaders of the nation. From their kind came the Galilean Carpenter. To be associated with them is to be in the greatest brotherhood in the world, and their lives as well as their words proclaim that they have more than a hearsay knowledge of God. These are the men who shame us and keep us steady.

Self-Consciousness

Popular and shallow success cults claim that they can teach men how to overcome their self-consciousness and thus be-

come dominating figures. It is hardly necessary to say that
this is not what we have in mind when we speak of curing
self-consciousness in the preacher. It is not merely learning
how to be nonchalant under trying circumstances or keeping calm before going into the pulpit. Unfortunately it is
neither as simple nor as discernible as that.

The temptation of self-consciousness is related to the experience of being "called" to the ministry. We are no longer
sure what we mean when we speak of this experience which
our fathers regarded as the essential element in the preacher's
original choice. We have seen many men who thought they
were called and who by their subsequent behavior proved
that either God's judgment was mistaken, or else they had
misunderstood Him. A generation that has gone all out for
God's activity in the so-called natural processes of life has
been suspicious of anything smacking of the supernatural
anywhere. There are preachers who have belittled the whole
idea of a special commission from God and they have insisted
that a man goes into the ministry just as he goes into any
profession. He has certain abilities and he chooses the ministry because it seems to give him the largest scope for them.
Therefore, such men conclude, give young men the usual
tests devised to reveal vocational fitness, and then if the tests
are not negative and the young man thinks he can face it, let
him become a minister.

Such an attitude, to me, is impossible. We may not have
experienced the vision of the cross in the sky or the burning
bush on the mountainside, but the real preacher rests more
and more on the miraculous certainty that God called him to
His work. All the implications of that choice are not apparent at the beginning, but they shine as the years give us eyes
to see and a spirit to appreciate. We have been set apart by
God to do a special work; of all the men He might have
called, He chose to exalt us with His commission. No man can
stay in the ministry and do his work with complete joy and

effectiveness unless he can rest on that. But woe unto us when we become self-conscious about our anointing.

The self-conscious prophet is the man whose ego makes him aware primarily of the prophet and his reputation rather than of the message and its effective presentation. It is the temptation to be more concerned with playing a part well than with being a channel for the Word of God. Nothing so destroys a man's ultimate effectiveness as to become entangled in his own ambitions.

It is not only a temptation of the preacher. Henry Adams writes:

> No man, however strong, can serve ten years as schoolmaster, priest, or senator, and remain fit for anything else. All the dogmatic stations in life have the effect of fixing a certain stiffness of attitude forever as though they mesmerized the subject.[7]

Our only quarrel with Henry Adams would be in regard to his insistence that no man can escape this corrosion. Granted that it takes almost a miracle to do it, still any man who is aware of the danger of his station can find a strength not his own to prevent his own mesmerizing. Richard Baxter, for example, gives us the necessary suggestion: "The work may be God's and yet we may do it, not for God, but for ourselves. I confess I feel such continual danger on this point, that if I do not watch, lest I should study for myself, rather than for Christ, I should soon miscarry."

All of those who talk blithely about "absolute honesty" had better come to the humble position where any man knows that absolute honesty is not possible for him or for anyone else. We are not in the ministry very long before we are aware that this is true:

> We are sincerely aware of God and of His call and Commission, but we are also, when we go into the pulpit, very conscious of ourselves being aware of God and of His call and

---

7 Adams, *The Education of Henry Adams,* Random House, 1931, 102.

commission. We are like those tiresome people who do genuinely admire the sunset, but when they speak of it, you know at once that, in addition they admire themselves admiring the sunset.[8]

A friend said to me one time in referring to one of my colleagues: "His prayers are not for me. He prays within himself and for himself." What he meant was that this man tends to wallow in his own emotions as an end in themselves. There are hymns like that and we will do well to ignore them. The service of worship is not set up for people to revel in their subjective feelings, but to worship God. Let the preacher remember that especially, for if any man in the sanctuary is in danger of falling into this pit, he is the man.

The self-conscious preacher soon runs dry for he has no source of supply except himself. Even if he studies and reads adequately, there is a golden extra which can come only from God. The artist in other fields comes to experience that baptism of inspiration which springs from where he knows not. Gamaliel Bradford wrote:

> It is the testimony of all who have made great art and have at all analyzed the process of making it, that something enters in and possesses them far more than mere superficial consciousness or effort. You sit down to your task quite hopeless, discouraged, incapable. Then suddenly, from you know not where, out of the depths of the subconscious, out of the inherited memory of the ages, the power comes upon you, and you speak, or appear to speak, with the tongues of angels.[9]

And there is no man who should expect this to happen so much as the preacher, for if he has been called to proclaim the Gospel, then he can be sure that God too is responsible for his preparation and message.

When we begin to prepare, consciously, a "great" sermon, we are in danger. Usually that means that a special occasion

---

8 Farmer, *The Servant of the Word*, Scribner's, 1942, 109.
9 Bradford, *Life and I*, Houghton Mifflin, 1928.

is approaching and if we do particularly well, many important people will be impressed. Much better it is to preach the
best sermon possible every week and follow some thought-
through program which will give the congregation a balanced diet. Remarque said in an article on writing that it is
better to write a bad novel than to try to write a perfect one
and then not do it. If we have it in us to preach a great sermon, that is fine, but we had better aim at preaching a true
sermon and one that people need to hear.

Boleslavsky in discussing acting said that the actor should
think not so much of the part as the author's conception of
the part. That is, the actor is not free to create a part for
himself only, but he must so understand the mind of the
author that he makes his particular part fit into the larger
whole of the play, even as the author had conceived it. The
implication of this for the preacher is important. It is not
for me to create a special part for myself but to seek humbly
to know what God had in mind for me to do and what His
plot demands of me. I shall find that only by seeking for a
comprehension of the mind of the Author and thus forgetting
myself.

The great preacher without self-consciousness cannot be
denied. He has the power of ten egocentric men who are
always stumbling over their own pride. Said David Hume
speaking of John Brown of Haddington: "That's the man for
me, he means what he says; he speaks as if Jesus were at his
elbow." We shall never quite succeed in this business until
we can say with Paul: "For to me to live is Christ," [10] and
thus bring everything into the light of his spirit. If we can
do that, we shall be able even to lay our self-consciousness
there and be rid of it. A young minister accused of bringing
too much strange material into his sermons was championed
by one of the elders in these words: "It wouldn't be reason-

---

10 Philippians 1:21.

able to expect old-fashioned sermons from a young man, and
I would count them barely honest. I'm not denying that he
goes far afield, and takes us to strange lands when he's on his
travels, but you will acknowledge that he gathers many treas-
ures, and he always comes back to Christ."

This, it seems to me, is the right word—we must "always
come back to Christ." We must hold that vision before the
church we serve. For the church must think of itself not as
the object of the preacher's service, but as a body under his
leadership to serve our Lord. The self-conscious preacher can
be healed if he becomes engrossed in holding before his
people Jesus Christ, and saying to them: "Let us together do
all we can for him." I am not to be served, but neither am I
a lackey to do for my laymen what they ought to do through
the Church. They were called to their ministry even as I am
called to mine. Together, we forget everything else except
the central calling of Christ to his service.

A minister of New Haven during the British occupation
was ordered to pray for the King. His prayer was as follows:
"O Lord, bless thy servant, King George, and grant unto him
wisdom; for Thou knowest, O Lord, he needs it." Such men
as that cannot be ordered by any other man, for they stand as
messengers of God, knowing that their orders come from Him
only. Unself-conscious preachers say with the Apostles: "We
must obey God rather than men."

If any man does not *have* to preach, let him do something
else, or he will have a miserable time of it. But if there is
no choice involved and if he knows that for better or worse
there is no other profession for him except the ministry,
then he is in a position to forget self. This is what Paul
learned and he, who could have been the most self-centered
of men, finds freedom through his conception of his calling.
He writes: ". . . for woe is unto me, if I preach not the
gospel. For if I do this of mine own will, I have a reward:
but if not of mine own will, I have a stewardship intrusted

to me." [11] Real freedom comes to the preacher when he learns to look toward God and not toward himself.

Plagiarism

The preacher is fortunate in that nothing is beyond the boundaries of his concern. In our blindness we have tried to make religion merely one interest among many, but in actual practice we learn that as long as we are dealing with life, we are dealing with religion, for religion is our total view of things. It has been pointed out rightly that if the Jews had played baseball, the rules of the game would have been in the Old Testament.[12] They thought religiously, which means they saw life as a whole—as a religious thing. Whatever the contemporary spirit may be, the preacher soon learns how to see all of experience as the raw stuff for his messages. To be on the constant search for material to be woven into the sermon pattern is to be like a hound always on the scent of the game being pursued; it is to have what someone called "the homiletic mind."

All of this is clear enough, but what is not so clear is our use of material which comes from others, and that is practically all of the material we use. The young preacher begins with the rather high ideal of preaching only his own message. Very good, until he learns that every time he thinks he has an original idea, he discovers later that many other men had the same idea, they defined it with greater clearness, and they presented it with superior effectiveness. It begins to dawn upon him that if he is to be an effective preacher he must depend on other men and lean on other sources than his own. Being a sensitive and honest person, he worries over using material and not giving credit for it. Yet preaching with a constant stream of quotations and references is not

11 I Corinthians 9:16–17.
12 Babson, Zuver, *Can These Bones Live?* Harper, 1945, 12.

preaching at all. What to do? If only we could do as the schoolboy did and simply define "plagiarist" as "a writer of plays."

Temptation finds us here when we try to make our material seems to be ours, even at the risk of dishonesty. We do it often by trying to put into personal form the illustration that was observed by or happened to someone else. Such was the case reported to me of a prominent preacher who told a story as a personal happening, but my informer discovered the same story in almost the same language imbedded in the writings of a man long since dead. It is not that this has done so much harm in itself as that the whole structure of a man's ministry has doubt cast over it. "He that is faithful in a very little is faithful also in much: and he that is unrighteous in a very little is unrighteous also in much [13] is a rather general feeling.

Sometimes this fear of borrowing drives a man to be too personal in his preaching and to fill his sermons with family allusions until the congregation becomes sick and tired of the preacher and all his relations. In this matter it is much better to err on the side of restraint. It is very questionable that the tendency to transform a religious meeting into an orgy of confession ought to be copied by the preacher in his pulpit.

Let us be sensible about it. Great men have always borrowed from others, as for example the Prophets. Jesus came bearing the great heritage of the Old Testament. Homer and Shakespeare found and used material from innumerable sources. Remember Kipling's words:

> When 'Omer smote 'is bloomin' lyre,
> He'd 'eard men sing by land and sea;
> An' what he thought 'e might require
> 'E went an' took—the same as me!

---

[13] Luke 16:10.

The market-girls an' fishermen,
.The shepherds an' the sailors, too,
They 'eard old songs turn up again,
But kept it quiet—same as you.

They knew 'e stole; 'e knew they knowed,
They didn't tell or make a fuss,
But winked at 'Omer down the road,
An' 'e winked back—the same as us.[14]

Material which has really found us and struck an answering note in our minds is never the same anyway, and we can be sure that the something added makes it ours. To be as honest as we can and never be guilty of the sin of pretense is a good rule. Or to put it in another way: We should use another man's material in such a way that if we knew he was listening to us, we would not be embarrassed. Anything less than this is not enough, and anything more than this is not necessary.

We have indicated a few of the major temptations of the ministry, but by no means have we exhausted the list. Nor will every man have the same temptations as every other man. But the preacher who never allows himself to forget that when he is talking to sinners, he is talking to himself, and when he is offering salvation from sin through Christ, he ought to be the first to stretch out for it, will be in the mood for God to help him. Our example is the Apostle who said that he made his body his slave "so that after I have called others to the contest I may not be disqualified myself." [15]

In another place it was suggested that it is a good thing to get into a routine when it comes to preparing sermons. I

---

[14] "When 'Omer Smote 'is Bloomin' Lyre," Preface to the "Barrack Room Ballads" in *The Seven Seas*. Copyright, 1893, 1894, 1896, 1905, 1933, by Rudyard Kipling. Used by permission of Mrs. George Bambridge, Doubleday & Company, Inc., The Macmillan Company of Canada, Ltd., and A. P. Watt & Son, London.

[15] I Corinthians 9:27 (Goodspeed).

cannot help but feel that the same is true when we are planning our devotional life. So many things get crowded out of the busy preacher's life that sometimes he awakens to the disturbing truth that he is urging his people to do what he does not find time to do himself. At some time during the day (for me it is the first thing in the morning) every preacher needs to have a time reserved for quietness and prayer. A half-hour spent in the presence of God pays such tremendous dividends that only a fool talks about lack of time for it. And the great thing about it is not only that one does one's work better and with less nervous tension, but that by giving the grace of Christ its opportunity to search us and try us, we can be cleansed of the peculiar sins which are ours.

It would be impossible to make a survey and discover the relationship between a man's devotional life and his success in the ministry. I suspect that there are men who have high places in the Church who do not practice the presence of God. But I am also sure that back of the message that probes and heals there is the self-searching and sincerity which comes only from devotional quietness. Some men will want a private shrine, symbols, and perhaps a book like *The Temple* by W. E. Orchard, to help them. Others will prefer only the privacy of their study and silence. But every man will need those moments when he opens his heart to God and waits for the still small voice, using the method that best fits his need. To leave this out is to court almost certain disaster.

If we were to list ten commandments for preachers, they might contain at least the following warnings:
1. Thou shalt not preach for any approval but God's.
2. Thou shalt not preach with one ear to the cash register, or bow before any idol.
3. Thou shalt not neglect thy personal devotions.
4. Remember the sacred places in thy life and keep them holy.

5. Honor thy colleague's success but covet not his style or his manners.
6. Thou shalt do nothing to kill the respect of thy people.
7. Thou shalt not make thy speaking a substitute for being.
8. Thou shalt not steal another man's material or congregation.
9. Thou shalt not exaggerate or in any way be false to the truth.
10. Thou shalt not become professionalized but remember always that thou art a servant.

PART TWO

THE MESSAGE: TIMELESS AND
CONTEMPORARY

VII

THE TENSION
OF MEETING

*". . . and a voice came out of
the heavens."*

Mark 1:11

The Baptism of Jesus differs in details in the separate
accounts and has been subject to considerable theological
controversy through the years. But the central significance
can hardly be doubted and the essential meaning of the
experience seems plain. It is the launching of the public
ministry of Jesus and it begins with a voice from God speaking directly to him, giving him assurance of the ultimate
triumph of his mission and promising divine support.

This is not referred to again by Jesus but it is not too much
to say that his whole ministry rests upon the assumption
that God meets men and speaks to them. His ethics are built
upon it and his promises and demands have no meaning
apart from this fundamental experience. According to Jesus,
religion is meeting, and the experience of religion is being
confronted and probed by a Person who meets men in terms
of personal will. The Christian religion is so saturated with
this understanding that it finally dawns upon us that to
deny it means to destroy Christianity.

Yet we have been denying it. The tremendous influence of
science and the unwarranted conclusions which have been
drawn from its premises have weakened our belief in Christianity's personal philosophy. Evolutionism, humanistic
optimism, and a naturalistic determinism have been spreading into the thought processes of the West. Thinking that
the only way to save Christianity was to make it acceptable

to this spirit, the Church has tended to minimize all in its faith that did not agree with it, and magnify all that could be interpreted in harmony with it. The result has not been a happy one. We have only produced a sort of secularized naturalism without much power, and not truly Christian. So far as our faith is concerned, God acts, He speaks, and He meets us.

The Christian Church's worship of size and its transformation into a business institution have made it particularly susceptible to this pagan, depersonalizing tendency. The preacher begins to see his people not as persons for whom Christ died and to whom God speaks through him, but as possible chairmen for committees, neutralizers for a troublesome brother, or large subscribers in the next money-raising campaign. The Church becomes not a fellowship but an organization, and the minister is not a shepherd of souls but a manipulator. How many churches there are where no one believes any more that Jesus spoke of a real experience when he said, "For where two or three are gathered together in my name, there am I in the midst of them." [1] How many ministers have hesitated during the past years to declare that God meets us and reveals His will to us!

There have been several reasons for our attempt to interpret Christianity in something else besides personal categories. An astronomer is reported to have said after turning away from his telescope, "This does away with a six-foot God; you cannot shake hands with the Creator of *this*." Nor can you speak to Him, we have said, nor can we expect Him to speak to us. For we have felt that it makes God less if we believe that He would either take the time or be interested in communicating with men. We have (mistakenly I believe) associated communication with an immature, anthropomorphic concept of Deity.

---

1 Matthew 18:20.

Then we have been so intrigued with the rational approach that we have paid scant attention to anything not confinable within it. The religious promptings of our natures when in conflict with our desire for rational enlightenment have not fared very well. We have often denied things with our minds which our hearts have proclaimed are true. We have been suspicious of our hearts. But it is just as easy to be misled by rationalism.

Virginia Woolf wrote:

> If you say to the public with sufficient conviction, "all women have tails and all men humps," it will actually learn to see women with tails and men with humps, and will think it very revolutionary and probably improper if you say, "Nonsense. Monkeys have tails and camels humps. But men and women have brains, and they have hearts; they think and they feel," —that will seem to it a bad joke, and an improper one into the bargain.[2]

She goes on to point out that Mr. Bennett is an example of many writers who approach the description of character by describing environment, background, and everything except daring to describe a real person.

Then, in a time when power has been our siren call, we have not been anxious to recognize anything like the voice of conscience in society. Since God's voice is always that, it has been most convenient for us to get rid of it, or at least muffle its tones, by denying its reality. Back of much of the modern anti-Semitism there is this attempt to deny what would be an embarrassment to the will for power, as Van Paassen pointed out.[3] We do not try to shout God down; we pretend His voice is only the sound of the wind. We even write our histories without referring to Him and we interpret events as if He never succeeded in effecting them.

---

[2] Woolf, "Mr. Bennett and Mrs. Brown," in Fadiman, *Reading I've Liked,* Simon & Schuster, 1945.

[3] Van Paassen, *Days of Our Years,* Dial, 1940.

Triumph of the Non-Personal

The Hebrew-Christian tradition holds at its center the confidence that men are at the same time very far from and very near to God. His ways are not our ways, but His word is intelligible to us. We have enough of His likeness to be able to understand something of His purposes and something of His communication to us. But if we deny that, then everything goes wrong.

The Nazi doctrine of the state as primary and the individual as valuable only in terms of his usefulness to the state becomes a nightmare when its full implications begin to appear. What horrible things men can do to men if they doubt that every man is potentially, at least, an instrument of God's will. The Marxist's willingness to subordinate the individual to the class results in a justification for the liquidation (our hypocritical term for murder) of any group which stands in the way of the triumph of the proletariat.

The social or political system that has no answer for personal questions leaves empty the most significant realms of life. Much as it would simplify many of our problems, men are neither able nor willing to negate their personal destinies for the sake of a deified state. That they will often sacrifice their lives for a cause is true, but it must be a free gift and an open option on their part. Thus Koestler relates that after hours of speeches at a Communist writers' congress describing the brave new world being constructed, one man asked, "And what about the man who is run over by a tramcar?" There was no answer but only a painful silence until someone finally replied, "In a perfect socialist transport system, there would be no accidents." And religion is supposed to be an opiate! No one could be satisfied with such an answer, and when the non-personal assumes supremacy over men, they must either decide to become less than men or be driven to madness.

"All vision is become unto you as the words of a book that is sealed," wrote Isaiah. Once started down the road to the denial of personal values and rights, a blindness comes over men so that they cannot understand their tragedy or analyze their sickness. They move by indirection as if they were afraid to face directly their need. The time comes when they give power to anyone with a pleasant bedside manner, but turn from anyone who might honestly diagnose the disease. Even our very ethics become impotent and we do not know how to repent.

In the nineteenth century people did not want moral values destroyed but they wanted them independent of God. But in the twentieth century, not even the moral values are respected or desired. Is it merely an accident or a coincidence that the divorcing of moral values from God results in the ultimate denial of the values themselves? The Christian answer is an emphatic "no!" It is on the contrary inevitable, for moral values are rooted in God's nature and men are not capable of holding them up apart from Him.

It is distressing how quickly literature becomes cheap and dirty when it loses its sense of a God who meets us, and looks at men from the standpoint of mere naturalism. It is not that literature becomes vulgar when it is concerned with certain aspects of life, as sex, for example. The Bible deals with sex and so do many of our great novels. It is not merely a matter of writing about certain kinds and conditions of men that makes literature unsavory. Great literature has never dealt only with the nice people who speak in genteel and refined manner. No, it is neither the subject matter nor the kind of characters written about that separates literature into the good and the bad. It is whether or not the author can see beyond the natural into the realm of the personal. In the words of Chesterton: "What is natural tends to become unnatural unless it is redeemed by what is supernatural."

This is the reason that no mechanical rules of censorship are ever quite satisfactory. For a book may contain no bad words and no intimate situations, and still be degrading. Or it may give the natural speech of uncultured people and approach all of life with a disarming frankness, and be ennobling. It is as if we could touch nothing without soiling it unless the natural functions of life are redeemed by the tension of meeting God.

The very best that literature can do when it moves outside the realm of the personal is to create abstractions instead of persons. Evelyn Waugh in commenting on his best seller *Brideshead Revisited* said,

> I have already shaken off one of the American critics, Mr. Edmund Wilson, who once professed a generous interest in me. He was outraged (quite legitimately by his standards) at finding God introduced into my story. I believe that you can only leave God out by making your characters pure abstractions. . . . So in my future books there will be two things to make them unpopular: a preoccupation with style and the attempt to represent man more fully which, to me, means only one thing, man in his relation to God.[4]

Whenever we face life in its concreteness, and great literature does that, then we meet God.

A cartoon in the St. Louis *Post-Dispatch* by Fitzpatrick showed a hand writing in large letters: "War Guilt Is Personal." Underneath there was the caption: "A New Era in International Law." True it is that the new era in all of life awaits our return to the sense of the personal in all relationships. For this can bring all of our life into relationship with God and He can save us from the crimes that are committed and go unchallenged when no person is to blame.

Yet, important as it is to see war guilt as personal, the peace continues to deteriorate because we are led by men who continue to believe that the world can be salvaged on

[4] *Life,* April 8, 1946.

the basis of non-personal values. Our real faith is still in materialism. Robert Louis Stevenson on one of his voyages to the South Seas told about a terrific storm that frightened all the passengers. One man finally went out on deck and watched the captain pace the bridge, calm and undisturbed. He came back to the cabin where the passengers were huddled together and said to them: "I have seen the captain's face and all is well." The race is kept steady and confident during its times of storm and stress when its leaders have a sense of human destiny as bound up with the will of God. Out of this there is born faith which is sufficient to weather the storm. To put this in another way—the only answer to our problem is the religious experience of being found by God.

The Meeting Experience

The Christian begins with the rather simple proposition that, God being what He is, He has made us as we are, created for fellowship with one another and through one another with Him. Once this human characteristic is properly appreciated, we begin to explore its implications and we discover that God offers His whole Self to our whole selves, as the late Archbishop of Canterbury, William Temple, once put it. There is enough common testimony of this central experience from the saints, the poets, and the careful Christian observers of all times and all places to make its denial almost absurd. The great Christians became poets, as they must be, in order to describe this experience at all adequately.

Chinanpin, the Chinese artist, made his students paint the orchid plant many times and was still dissatisfied with the results. Finally he explained that though the leaves droop toward the earth, they long to point to the sky. He called it "cloud-longing" and he insisted that the artist must feel that before he can give the living quality to the flower. That is a parable of human life. While we are of the earth, we long for the realm of heaven, and until we understand that God-longing has its consummation in meeting, we cannot understand man and the implications of this central Christian experience.

It has been said that, while this may be recognized, still the object of the desire may be an abstraction which is more than man but less than God. We should remember the schoolboy's definition of an abstract noun as "the name of something which does not exist, like honor or truthfulness." As a matter of experience we learn that the old division of things into essence and existence does not represent two ways of being but two aspects of being and they cannot be separated except arbitrarily in the imagination. The fear that God as Person is a less sophisticated concept than God as a principle, or a trend, or a drift, or an abstraction, or an essence, should now be set aside as the conclusion of an approach that is shallow and one-sided. An abstract idea hanging between heaven and earth clearly cannot confront my mind with any claim, unless it is rooted in some concrete reality.

Man is conditioned to a world of personal relations and a personal order that leads to God. Many a child seems to know that from the beginning, and never drifts into any kind of doubt about it. Even savages have their taboos, speaking of someone above them who makes his demands and has a right to do so. Who are people trying to please when obviously they are not trying to please either themselves or other people? To say it is merely a principle does not at all explain the sense of personal guilt they feel when they fail, or the sense of joyous triumph when they partly succeed. Even in the very protests against the divine claim and the attempt to be free from it, there is the shrillness and the defiance of children rebelling against the inevitable.

Yet if we are stubbornly wayward, still God meets us as individuals or as a society at the edge of things. When at last we stand at the abyss, having grown weary of inventing gadgets to help us get through the hours of the day, we may see something beyond ourselves. For like Dorian Grey, men can look at themselves only for a limited time before they are driven to despair. Then as we seek to escape this, we are driven to listen with desperation for His reassuring word.

When Nathan confronted David with his sin and his guilt, he spoke this direct word: "Thou art the man." It was the genius of Israel's religion that the Prophet spoke for God not only to the peasant but to the king. And as is so often the case, God met the king in his shame. The whole experience of being ashamed leads directly to the God who is a Person and who will not be put off. My moral failure is something much different from my intellectual failure. If a man makes a mistake in judgment or a mistake because he lacked knowledge, that is something quite different from making an immoral choice. For the wrong choice has to do with my being a person, and I feel that I failed someone who had a right to expect better of me.

Many a man is saved by guilt, and the beginning of a better life is often that moment when a man confesses, "I was ashamed." But why am I ashamed? If no one knows about it except myself, why am I still ashamed? Does an abstract principle create shame within me? It seems to me that whenever one talks about being ashamed, he is talking about personal relations, and if there is that within the cosmic processes that makes me experience shame, then there is that within the cosmic processes which is personal.

The very concept of faith implies personal relationship. If man is saved by faith, and the great leaders of religion have never doubted it, then he is the kind of creature who finds his salvation by a response to Someone who is making a demand upon him. In the impersonal relations of life, it is only knowledge and ability that count. But in the personal relations these things are secondary to faith, trust, and response.

This is why man never finds his security in the material values of life. Economic safety, wealth, power, or even alcohol are often the objects of man's search for safety or at least for relief from worry. It has become trite to say that these things do not provide it, and cannot provide it. Still, there is a certain amount of truth in saying that the man who staggers up the street drunk is on a mistaken quest for God. At least he is looking for something which he can never have until he finds God, and the cheap substitute simply reveals the undying hunger of men for assurance. Being what we are, we will never be satisfied until we meet One beyond ourselves. Augustine's words say it best: "Thou hast made us for thyself and our hearts are restless until they find rest in thee."

One of my friends was talking with her grandson one evening about God, and after some discussion the boy was silent for a time and then he said, "We walk down the street and suddenly along comes God." Indeed He does! Sometimes He comes along in retribution or suffering, and sometimes He is there in joy and triumph. But He comes along and the Christian learns to expect Him around the next corner or at the next stopping place. The meeting will not be a matter of receiving precise instructions for the next stage of the journey, but it will be a renewal of confidence that comes when you meet a friend. When God comes along, too many people fail to recognize Him because the sign of His presence is that our hearts burn within us. Hardly ever does He tell us how to close the pending deal, or make a financial profit, or get our way over another.

The meeting is not always of a spectacular nature, nor does it often seem to us miraculous. When a husband has been away for many months to the wars where he has walked in danger, his home-coming is one of those marvelous, precious moments that can never be forgotten or described by either husband or wife. But it is impossible to make every meeting at the close of the day like that. When the husband comes home from his office or his business, the wife will not greet him just the same way as she did on that occasion of his return from overseas. But a real marriage always has the underlying sense of that special meeting, so that without fanfare or external drama its quality permeates even the daily relationships.

So with our meeting God! Not often will we be called to the mountain to receive the laws, or to be transfigured before our friends. In the words of the epigram: "One hour of Transfiguration to forty days in the wilderness is the normal average." But the simpler experiences will speak to us of the special meetings, and we will find the quiet encounters with Him partaking of the joy of the great ones. Jesus said, "I say unto you, that even so there shall be joy in heaven over one sinner that repenteth, more than over ninety and nine righteous persons, who need no repentance." [5] But the ninety and nine, remembering their own return, learn to live under the joy of that moment, and the quiet, continual meetings are all colored by it.

The Claim

Fred Clark, national commander of a semi-fascist organization called the Crusaders, once said that he had no objection to teachers' talking about conditions in the Soviet Union if they always made clear that conditions were bad. He was not the first or the last to believe in freedom of speech within certain clearly defined limits.

Something of that same spirit governs our approach to God. We are willing for Him to speak if we can be sure that He will not demand too much from us or tend to upset our comfortable habits. So we are the kind of creatures who pray for Him to speak to us, but if He does, we will not listen. There is the inescapable feeling that if God speaks, He will

---

[5] Luke 15:7.

set up the tension of a claim upon us. Even those who take refuge in regarding the claim as coming from society find that it comes from the sense of what society *ought* to be, which I think means God.

This fear is sometimes alleviated by making God a rich uncle whose rather sentimental favoring of justice and truth can be overruled by a well-aimed and timely prayer. Like the gods of the Greeks, we make Him interesting and weak like ourselves and we have the same affectionate regard for Him that we have for any nice old gentleman who is always good for a gift. There is so much of our religion that is sheer magical romance and good for nothing but to shed a pious light about our prosperous days. One blast of adversity smashes the whole business and we wallow in self-pity until things improve and we take up again where we left off.

But the real Christian experience is an assurance that God knows all about us, how much we earn, what we do with our money, and what we are like when we are at our worst. How can God know all about me and why should He be concerned about me? We can make it look ridiculous philosophically, but we can never escape the feeling that it is true. And always there is the certainty that He puts a claim on me that will either drive me to restless anxiety or exalt me to the fulfillment of my best self. It is not just facing a law; it is facing a Judge. Two little girls were looking at a portrait of Queen Victoria in her royal robes. One asked the other, "What is she doing?" And the other replied, "She isn't doing anything. She is just reigning." But God won't just reign. He reaches out with an imperative demand that will not let me go.

We are wrong, therefore, when we think we can separate this meeting experience from the tension of a demand and a judgment. The comfort of our faith comes from the cross, which is at once suffering and triumph, consolation and demand. For as Dr. Herbert Farmer of Cambridge has pointed out more than once, there can be no comfort for mature persons aside from a claim. A generation that separates the two will shun the cross and regard evil as an illusion. There is no more certain sign than that of spiritual sickness.

It is this quality of the central experience of Christianity that prevents it from ever becoming sentimental and mushy. No real Christian ever talks about forgiveness as if it were something cheap and easy. The kind of person who says that it is God's business to forgive us, and we should take it without too much ado, is the kind of person who never experienced it. For it is a terrible, awful thing, to be forgiven. The defenses are all down and a soul stands stripped of its pride. The only possible comfort in the forgiveness of God is to surrender completely to His Will, which more times than not will insist on our taking up the cross. But by saying yes to that, we discover our healing.

Dr. Emil Brunner says that "it is much more comfortable to have a pantheistic philosophy than to believe in a Lord God. . . . A God who is neuter makes no claim. He simply allows himself to be looked at." Whatever else the experience of meeting God may be, it has never been primarily relaxation. That in some strange way the experience brings peace is true, but it is always the peace of tension. It is a fearful thing to meet God and we shrink from it, for He takes us to the Resurrection morning by way of the cross.

Fortunately for us, we do not have to approach this meeting without guidance. The extremist who believes that every man must begin from the beginning in his religious experience is like the man who refuses to accept any authority in any field. To him we should reply as did the Ph.D. candidate to a professor who was unnecessarily exacting in his criticism of the footnotes: "I did not discover America, I took it second hand from Christopher Columbus." We shall take much in this matter from the Bible. The Bible preacher who can preach not only about the Bible but from within it has the power to bring this direct testimony in a way that makes the path to God plainer. It cannot be said too much that when we are trying to lead men into the mystery of God's dealing with men, the Bible is our best guide.

The attitude of a generation toward the Bible is in direct relation to its attitude toward the central meaning of Christianity. When we believe that Christianity's main message is one of confidence in a non-personal process, then the Bible is not only irrelevant—it is a nuisance. Long before Hitler, a generation which had put its trust in the starry heavens above and the moral law within as the best indications of God felt some embarrassment and confusion in finding a place for the records and pronouncements of an obscure Semitic tribe. Only when we are willing to accept the Bible's primary insights is its effectiveness given a free reign.

This effectiveness, in my judgment, is due to the Bible's power of bringing men face to face with God at every turning. An English preacher once suggested that it would be well to read the thirteenth chapter of I Corinthians and substitute the word "God" for "love," and thus read: "God suffereth long, and is kind; God envieth not," etc. There is a sense in which the Bible puts God in the place of every attempt on our part to substitute some impersonal, mechanistic concept. Thus does it bring into sharp focus the dramatic, purposeful nature of our universe and rescue us from the temptation to dehumanize ourselves and our world.

The Bible shows us God confronting us as sinners in terms of judgment and punishment. It shows Him facing us with our need for something beyond our human horizons when we would be cleansed and forgiven. It reveals One who will not let us forget our accountability, destroying our little efforts to believe in behaviorism or fatalistic helplessness. But at last it shows us power offered by God through Jesus Christ our Lord.

The glorious climax of the Bible, which is God meeting

us through a Person, becomes a more wonderful thing with every passing generation. A soldier on leave, after two years at the front in the First World War, was killed in the back areas by a long-distance gun. His last words were: "Isn't that just like God?" But as an English preacher remarked, he would never have said: "Isn't that just like Jesus Christ?" [6] That which keeps us from losing sight of God's personal care for men is Jesus, and he is our protection against the cynicism of the mere bigness of the universe. It is Jesus Christ, and he crucified, who keeps us centered on the God who meets us.

God in Christ knocks at the door of each man's life and then gives him no rest until He has been admitted into every corner of that life. We may put it in different ways, but at the heart of our faith there is the central assurance which was expressed as well as it can be said by St. Paul: "God was in Christ reconciling the world unto himself. . . ." [7]

A religion that takes history seriously, as Christianity does, must find in history the field of the divine activity of God. Someone said that God is like the Supreme Court in that He never deals with hypothetical cases. History is to Christianity a revelation of the actual dealing with actual cases by God. So history becomes something more than a series of happenings or a blind interpretation of events. It becomes a tradition and

Tradition, as Masaryk understood it, was not a sum total of habits, conventions, customs and folklore. Tradition to him was a covenant between fathers and sons, mutual pledge of allegiance to what our conscience regards as true and just, noble and right. Tradition was to him a responsible continuance of the struggle for the highest ideals and aspirations of our history, a continuous reaffirmation of our loyalty to the great cause of truth and righteousness. [8]

[6] *Religion in Life*, Longmans, Green, 1935, 2.
[7] II Corinthians 5:19.
[8] Hromadka, *Doom and Resurrection*, Madrus House.

Which is to say, history too is a place where God meets us.

All of this for some people is easy to experience and is never questioned. This is not true of all men. Words are simply marks on a page until we learn to read, and there are a considerable number of people who can never learn to read, even though in other activities they may be fairly competent. I had two friends one time who played chess together as they rode along in a car, keeping the board, the pieces, and the moves clear in their heads. Not in a hundred years could I learn to do that. George Antheil, the composer and pianist, says that he can pick up a score and as he reads it actually hear the music. To some of us, that is in the realm of magic and beyond our comprehension.

So in this matter of meeting God and hearing Him speak, I am confident that it is much simpler for some than it is for others. But for all men it is primarily a matter of recognition. Once we have broken down the prejudice which our age has raised against it, experience will follow. In the meantime, we may learn to live expectantly, knowing that sensitive spirits, the Bible, Jesus, and history are united in their testimony that at the heart of the Christian experience there is the tension of meeting God.

Implications

Now all of this has very special implications for the function of preaching. Unless we have lost all sense of the sacredness of our task, we do not refer to it as a job, but as a calling. We do not mean, I think, that something happened at a particular time, once and for all. We mean that as long as we listen, He will speak to us as well as through us. We preach because we believe we worship a living God who still has a word for men and will continue to inspire men to proclaim it. The Bible is not a closed book for us, and like John Robinson, we believe that there is still light to break forth from it. Our high calling is to be those who can hear

Him and then interpret His Word to men in their need.
We may not have read the latest book or practiced the latest
fad, but we have a sense of which way God Almighty is going
to move in the next fifty years, which Gladstone said was
the mark of a statesman. Certainly it is the mark of the
preacher.

If any man has been in a foreign country alone and with
no knowledge of the language, he begins to comprehend that
communication is just about the most important thing in the
world. He would have to consider long and carefully before
he would surrender the ability to hear in preference to some
other faculty. It is not too much to say that communication
with God is even more necessary to health and sanity. The
sobering truth is that there are many people who will hear
Him only as we speak for Him, and they will meet Him only
as we are able to introduce them.

In these days, most of us either dictate to our secretaries
or use a typewriter ourselves. But in those moments when
we must communicate with a friend concerning an intimate,
important, personal matter, we write to him by hand. If, as
in my case, the handwriting is atrocious, still we know that
when we must write personally, we dare not do it through
another person or even through a machine. We must actually
hold the pen and form the letters ourselves. So when God
would communicate something really important to men,
nothing can take the place of a person who alone can bring
His personal word to men. It was John's great affirmation
that God could bring His personal assurance to us only
through Jesus. There is, therefore, no comparable way for
men to hear saving truth but through persons, and that
means preachers.

This means also that abstract preaching is very bad preaching. How often the preacher wishes that God had made him
a poet that he might draw with sharp outline the picture of
what he tries in vain to say. Or he longs for the spear thrusts

of the prophet that seem to penetrate straight to the heart of the situation. Perhaps we have not been given these special gifts, but at least we must not be content with the general and dull approach which characterizes theology and philosophy at their worst. Let us learn that we cannot speak about God effectively unless we have learned to convert our abstractions into concrete terms. We read that there are a thousand casualties, or 5 per cent of a population are starving, and we do not react because we see numbers and percentages instead of persons. Preaching ought to translate the meaningless generalities that leave us untroubled, into men, women, and little children whose suffering will break our hearts.

Even our social work carried on outside the realm of concrete cases results in a continuation of the depersonalizing processes which threaten our destruction. There is a case of a well-to-do woman who gave her afternoons to presiding over a nursery for the children of the poor. One day she discovered that she was looking after the children of the woman whom she had hired to look after her children while she did her social service. If we do not know what we are doing, there is just as much chance we are doing harm as good. To sponsor causes and promote uplift movements can become a sort of social disease unless we bring our efforts into the light of the purposes of God who meets us in one another and in Jesus. Woe unto us when we preach causes and not people.

One of the ways the preacher makes his message concrete is through the use of illustrations. In this matter we tend to fall into one of two pitfalls—either we use too many illustrations and our sermons are merely a string of stories, or else we do not use any and our discourse has no windows and no preciseness. As a means of clinching a point, or of holding the interest, it is necessary to show the meaning of the message in a particular instance. It is roughly true that every gen-

eral proposition needs at least one illustration of its implications, and usually more.

Illustrations should not be trite. If a preacher keeps up
his reading, he will not need to fall back on the old stories
that make a man inwardly groan when he sees them coming
at him again. Nor should they be drawn out or blown up,
for while it is necessary to indicate from time to time that
two times two equals four, there is no need to labor the point.
It will always be a temptation to strain a favorite illustration
in an effort to make it fit into next Sunday's sermon. This
never works; unless the illustration is right, it is worse than
none at all. We must develop the will power which will keep
the illustration until the right moment has arrived for it,
whether that comes next Sunday or a year from now. Personal
illustrations are like seasoning in that they add zest if used
sparingly but make the product indigestible if they are used
too much. On the whole it is better to leave them out altogether than to risk their over-use. But now and again they
will be as effective as anything a man can do, in making
God real.

Our best models will be the parables of Jesus for in them
we see how a great preacher makes unforgettable and unes-
capable a mighty truth. They were brief, with only one point,
and they threw light on a great idea. They made an abstraction like "God is love" find a man's spirit with wonder and
power, like a miracle. Our preaching will be in Jesus' tradition if each man leaves our service saying, "God met me at
this point today, and I never recognized Him there before."

Then, of course, the implication of this nature of our faith
is that we must preach for a decision. When a man meets
God, he has to decide something, for that eternal claim is
where freedom must make its choice. We do not need to feel,
I think, that every service must end with an altar call. Yet
our fathers were right in believing that no man has preached

who has not set up in each man's soul the tension of meeting God. What the decision is finally we may never know, but that any man should leave us feeling relaxed, unstrung, and at ease would mean that for him there was no meeting. The sermon is not a series of opening scenes but a drama that moves forward to a climax, which is that moment when my will has been challenged by His will. Because we cannot separate our message from our method, it is important that we should have always this central thing in our minds as we prepare to preach: At the heart of the Christian experience, God confronts each man with the tension of His claim.

VIII

WHO CAN BUT PROPHESY?

". . . the Lord Jehovah hath spoken."

Amos 3:8

When one looks at those giants of the Bible whom we have called *the Prophets,* he will be likely to feel that he can never aspire to be one of their number.

> Such knowledge is too wonderful for me;
> It is high, I cannot attain unto it.

Yet we who are called by His grace to bring His word to men through preaching have no choice. We are called to be prophets of the people and to the people. Our message is one of realistic criticism and it is ruthless in its blasting away of obstacles to the coming of the Kingdom.

The prophet is an interpreter of life in the light of the purpose of God. To him, history reveals that when men move toward God, they move toward the light, and when they move away from Him, they move toward the darkness. The prophet dares to prescribe for a sick society by seeing the sickness as a need for adjustment to the will of God. He pictures the future in terms of men's willingness or refusal to accept the demands of God. Sometimes he is mistaken about the future when he tries to describe it in too intimate detail, but he never doubts that the clue to history and the clue to the future is God.

I think the prophet is a man who is especially sensitive to the sin of idolatry and he excels in his ability to describe the contemporary idols. Always he is striving to bring men to the worship of the true God, while men are so easily led

147

to the worship of the idol. The prophet is the man chosen of
God to proclaim: "Thou shalt have no other gods before
me." So in every generation, Christian preachers are called
to describe the camouflaged idolatry of that day, proclaim
the destruction that will come to an idolatrous people, and
call men back to the worship of God. Facing the dark despair
of this moment, what preacher cannot feel the terrible compulsion that was upon Amos? "The lion hath roared," he
writes, "who will not fear? the Lord Jehovah hath spoken,
who can but prophesy?" (Amos 3:8)

We shall not stop the disintegration of our civilization by
making strikes illegal, or by building homes filled with
gadgets, or by using vitamins. All of this is merely trying to
heal a cancer by rubbing a salve on it. The more we try to
make our plans for the future on this basis, the more we
cry out for faith or morale. We betray the sad truth that we
have no faith and no confidence in the plans we are making.
We talk much about the need for religion, but we want a
religion that can wash us without getting us wet, which is
to say, a religion that will save us without changing us.

A ship crossing the Atlantic ran into a terrific storm and
one of the feminine passengers went to the captain asking,
"Captain, is there any danger?" "No, madam," replied the
captain, "not yet. The sailors are still swearing, but if they
start to pray, put on your life-belt." We still regard religion
as something to ward off special danger, but not as a way
of life. The process began with the deterioration of the
medieval world and the birth of the Renaissance. There is
a sense in which our main task is to get over the Renaissance.
This is not to say that we want to return to a medieval kind
of life. That is impossible even if it were desirable, but it
is to say that we are beginning to reap the inevitable results
of substituting the human, materialistic gods for Jehovah.
The Renaissance was a wrong turning. That it accomplished
much no one can deny, and that life is more comfortable

now than it was then is certainly true. But the time has come when we have to consider what science has done to us, as well as what it has done for us, and the extent to which it has meant the worship of idols.

The great study that has been made in our generation of the rise and fall of civilizations is *A Study of History* by Arnold Toynbee. In this six-volume work, which is not yet completed, Toynbee analyzes the disintegrations of civilizations and draws the main implications from the analysis. He talks about the "Schism in the Body Social" and he points out that back of all the surface signs of the disintegration there is the spiritual failure within. Some scholars believe that nothing can be done about this process, since societies are organisms and move inevitably through their youth and maturity to old age and death. Toynbee does not believe the process is irreversible, and Christians do not believe it either.

Yet, while most people are aware that all is not well, we cannot bring ourselves to be disillusioned with the way we follow and the values we hold dear. Even the war has not done that for us, and most leaders seem to assume that a little more of the same thing we have assumed signified progress will finally lead us out of the woods. The Church is not guiltless in this failure. The Church has itself burned incense before the idols of prosperity. Preachers have too often assumed that their message has to be adjusted to the contemporary philosophy. The priests of religion are often too deeply rooted in the *status quo* to be able to see clearly all that is involved. The task of the prophetic voice is to call our civilization to repentance, which means to re-establish the altar of God and remove the idols.

Our Lack of Unity

It is apparent intellectually to any man that this is *One World*. No one who reads can fail to see how closely related

we are, and speakers refer to this so often that it has become
as trite as the Golden Rule. World trade has extended widely
so that we are interdependent; communication is possible
with speed and efficiency. Distance has ceased to exist and
when we are told about the still further miracles ahead, we
have difficulty in keeping our imaginations pliable enough to
comprehend it. All of this should mean peace and prosperity.
At least that was the theory, and we were told that there
would be no room, in a world of international trade, for
war and destruction. It was said of the Dutch, for example,
that they would rather trade with a Turk who paid cash
than with a Presbyterian who asked for six months' credit.
What difference would it make if we had different religions
and ideologies? After all, business is business and where we
failed to be united religiously, the materialistic pursuits
would do the job.

Well, unfortunately "something went wrong." With all
of this accomplished, we seem as far from one world as ever.
The rivalries among the big nations are so real that they
must assure each other constantly how much they love each
other. No one is deceived. The business interests which were
to unite the world are often the very forces which sow distrust
and suspicion through competition. With all of our talking
with each other, we still fail to find a common ground. For
communication is a matter of the spirit and not of words.
We do not know how to communicate, we only know how
to propagandize.

Every unified society has found its unity in terms of the
spirit. Even the Holy Roman Empire, which, as some wit
has put it, was not holy, and was not Roman, and was not
an empire, was essentially a religious idea with its roots in
the Christian doctrine of the brotherhood of man and the
Fatherhood of God. And if it took a religious idea to hold
together the relatively simple societies of the past, will any-

thing less powerful hold together the complicated society of the West in the twentieth century? Let us make no mistake about this, religion is the one basis of unity any society can have, for it alone can bring all the activities of life into a meaningful oneness.

Unity means life, and the single aim is possible only when we are made one through the power of a living purpose. There is a sense in which science deals only with the dead, and philosophy can only seek reasons for what it observes. But real religion has within it the pulsing power of life for it witnesses to the God who acts. Men who are dead in all but the physical sense make known their condition by their vain attempts to live on a plane where there is no vision beyond their day-to-day existence. Their societies are revealed as dying things because they have no faith in anything beyond their own selfish welfare.

This lack of unity is apparent in individual lives lived apart from religion. Some of our outstanding psychologists are coming to see this. Jung, who has been consulted by many people seeking mental health, said that he had never counseled with a person thirty-five years of age or over whose problem was not ultimately that of finding a religious view of life. This word comes not from a man who is trying to promote a particular faith, but from a psychologist whose responsibility is to combine a mob of conflicting emotions, desires, and frustrations into a person.

It is all right to think of the world as a stage and each man playing his part, but there comes a time when we must ask ourselves who wrote the play? what kind of drama is it? and how is it going to end? Shall we think of the conclusion of the whole business as a whining farce, or as a triumphant tragedy? No man who considers his life, and, as Plato said, the unconsidered life is not worth living, does so without being driven to religion. If modern men are frustrated and frightened, it is owing finally to having given their real devotion to an idol instead of to God.

I have a great deal of sympathy for that woman whose daughter was about to take a course in physiology. She wrote to the high-school principal: "I don't want my Mary to learn no more about her insides." We know enough about our insides and the parts, but we do not know enough about that which will make us whole again. The unity of personal life as well as of social life is possible only with God as the center simply because that is the way men are. Therefore, let the Christian prophet declare that our search for unity is in vain until we return to God.

Our Ignorance of Human Life

When men set up the idols in the temple, they are moved by pride. Ahaz sought for more personal splendor in his reign, and set up an altar modeled after the pagan one at Damascus, setting aside in the shadows the altar of God. Antiochus Epiphanes, seeking healing for his wounded pride when he was turned back from Egypt by Rome, placed the Abomination of Desolation in the Temple. Rome could not stand having a rival loyalty beside the state, and so persecuted those Christians who refused to burn incense at the statue of the emperor. In modern times, we have turned to the pagan gods of materialism, because they flatter our egos and make us feel that we are entirely self-sufficient. There is truth in the old proverb which says, "Whom the gods would destroy, they first make mad." That madness is pride. The trend in recent times has been to sing, "Glory to man in the highest," in the phrase of Swinburne. Freed from old superstitions and at last aware of our power over nature, we have gaily followed Freud and his school, which proclaimed religion with its worship of God an illusion.

For Walt Whitman's seventieth birthday in 1889, Mark

Twain wrote him a letter on behalf of a committee of American men of letters. This is what he said:

> You have lived just the seventy years which are greatest in the world's history and richest in benefit and advancement to its peoples. These seventy years have done much more to widen the interval between man and the other animals than was accomplished by any of the five centuries which preceded them. What great births you have witnessed! The steam press, the steamship, the steel ship, the railroad, the perfect cotton gin, the telegraph, the phonograph, photogravure, the electrotype, the gaslight, the electric light, the sewing machine, and the amazing, infinitely varied and innumerable products of coal tar, those latest and strangest marvels of a marvelous age. And you have seen even greater births than these; for you have seen the application of anesthesia to surgery-practice, whereby the ancient dominion of pain, which began with the first created life, came to an end on this earth forever. . . . Yes, you have indeed seen much—but tarry for a while, for the greatest is yet to come. Wait thirty years, and then look out over the earth! You shall see marvels upon marvels added to those whose nativity you have witnessed; and conspicuous about them you shall see their formidable Result—man at almost his full stature at last!—and still growing, visibly growing while you look. . . . Wait till you see that great figure appear, and catch the far glint of the sun upon his banner; then you may depart satisfied, as knowing you have seen him for whom the earth was made, and that he will proclaim that human wheat is more than human tares, and proceed to organize human values on that basis. (Signed) Mark Twain.

And today, Walt Whitman must look down from the other world at the remains of concentration camps, at mothers suffering, at defeated, hopeless people, at Hiroshima, at starved children, at our veterans' hospitals for the physically and mentally destroyed, and perhaps he smiles, but in all probability he weeps. We have come a long way during the time since Whitman's death, but it has not been to man's "full stature at last."

What we did, of course, was to substitute man for God, which is another manifestation of idolatry. The deification of man came about when we decided that men were good and needed no power outside themselves for their salvation. We thought only ignorance was our enemy, and when we had destroyed that, then the golden age would be here. It is the old heresy which constantly manifests itself within the theology of the Christian Church. Thus far, the Church has been able to recognize it for the falsehood it is, but under the terrific impact of our actual accomplishments and the unlimited promises of the future, even preachers became deeply infested with it. Will Durant said the twentieth century discovered that knowledge is neutral. Christianity has always known that and the twentieth century has not really learned it yet. An inscription in the Nebraska State House says: "Eyes and ears are poor witnesses when the soul is barbarous." Human knowledge is destruction and not salvation, if the heart is evil.

The truth is that man is a sinner and can only find cleansing through God. Yet this is the very thing which the false god always denies. The Bible from the story of the Fall of Man in Genesis to Jesus' attack on the Pharisees is aware of the reality of sin and tells the story of what happens to men and societies when they deny it. Our modern time has so rebelled against this idea of man as sinner that it sees only an outgrown superstition when it is mentioned. To Western civilization it needs to be said in the words of Hosea to his people: "O Israel, return unto Jehovah thy God; for thou hast fallen by thine iniquity. Take with you words, and return unto Jehovah: say unto him, Take away all iniquity, and accept that which is good. . . ." (Hosea 14:1–2)

The late Lord Morley, though he never called himself a Christian, was one of the most upright men who ever rose to high office in the British government and was also a very shrewd observer of human life. He once criticized Emerson, our American optimist, because he said that Emerson had never really faced "that horrid impediment on the soul, which the Churches call sin, and which, by whatever name we call it, is a very real catastrophe in the moral nature of man." The difference between Christianity and other philosophies is its willingness to begin with the worst—the fact of sin in human nature.

It will seem like an extreme statement to many, but I believe that St. Paul knew more about human nature than many modern psychologists. Paul saw the desires of men and also their weakness. He learned that we must find a power not ourselves which will lead us in the way of righteousness. Behavioristic psychology in particular, and those schools which have been influenced by it, ask the wrong questions and so they always get the wrong answers. With all of our apparatus for experimentation, we lag behind the deep and true insights of Paul because he began not with hypothetical cases but with his own heart and his own need. He never taught the depravity of human nature, but he taught the powerlessness of human nature apart from God.

The fundamental sin is pride. Reinhold Niebuhr has revealed this as the Biblical doctrine and he had shed as much light on it for modern readers as any theologian. His suggestion that even when we become humble we get proud because we are humble is a clear understanding of this most subtle nature of sin. We so easily forget our limitations. So prone are we to pride that it usually takes a catastrophe to make us humble again. Only today we know that the next catastrophe may be so complete that salvation will not be possible for us, but only for some far-off generation that will salvage what little it can and begin anew.

Yet this sense of sin is not a degrading thing nor is it a creator of whiners. It is, on the contrary, that which preserves the balance of life and makes it possible to walk humbly with our God on the road to our real destiny. **G. K.**

Chesterton understood this clearly, and even in his detective stories the truth shines through. Thus, Father Brown, the canny priest, is visited by an American who tells him that in America they have decided he is the greatest detective in the world, and that his success is due to second sight. Father Brown is horrified at this idea and denies it emphatically. "I had thought out exactly how a thing like that could be done, and in what style or state of mind a man could really do it. And when I was quite sure that I felt exactly like the murderer myself, of course I knew who he was." When the American objects that this sounds morbid, the priest answers:

> "No man's really any good till he knows how bad he is or might be, till he's realized exactly how much right he has to all this snobbery and sneering, and talking about 'criminals' as if they were apes in a forest ten thousand miles away; till he's squeezed out of his soul the last drop of the oil of the Pharisees; till his only hope is somehow or other to have captured one criminal, and kept him safe and sane under his own hat."[1]

And the priest is right. Even as Adam and Eve were driven from the Garden of Eden because they aspired to be equal to God, so we shall be driven from our scientific, materialistic garden unless we humble ourselves, confess our sin, and worship God.

Real Foundations of Culture

In a time when many a thoughtful man feels that our culture is crumbling we are driven to a re-examination of the foundations of it. The number of books being written about civilization and its laws indicates our deep concern over our present precarious situation. Men like Spengler, Brooks Adams, Sorokin, Mumford, Mannheim, Toynbee, and a score of others are analyzing our society and trying to prescribe for its ills. A healthy society is not concerned about these things any more than really healthy people are willing

---

1 Chesterton, *The Secret of Father Brown*, Cassell, 1927, 13.

to define religion as physical health. Health is of deep concern only to the sick. But we are sick and hence we are trying to discover what is wrong.

For a good many decades now, we have been assuming that the essential of our civilization is techniques of control over the physical universe. When we talk about progress, we mean life that is more comfortable, travel that is faster, and work that includes less drudgery. It is amazing how we have turned our attention almost entirely to the outer world. The inner world is a no-man's-land for us, as if we feared to look at the emptiness within or perhaps worse, to look and become troubled by a vision of what we ought to be. We have made the manipulations of nature our chief interest and our chief skill.

The great changes in our life as compared to the earlier centuries are due to science. Whenever we boast of the marvels the modern world has achieved as compared to ancient times, we are paying tribute to science. The accomplishment is tremendous and no one would want to minimize the power that modern man has developed to affect his environment. It was perhaps to be expected that such a mighty influence would deeply affect our philosophy and our religion. It has seemed to us that at last we have found something that provides unlimited possibilities for tomorrow. The power and advantage we have over all other cultures has given us a picture of a future without a ceiling.

Yet, when all is said and done, we must affirm that the foundation of our culture is not science, but Christianity. This sounds like nonsense to many people, but the foundation of any culture is its religion and not its science. We rest our way of life on faith and belief so that the weakening of these intangible things means a deterioration which our physical skill is powerless to prevent. The so-called "new orders" shocked us so profoundly because they developed and used our science and our techniques, but they used them outside the framework of the Christian faith. We saw a way of life that used every available material resource with which we had grown so familiar and so proud, but there was sluffed off the underlying ethical ideas, rooted in our religion. There was eliminated openly the doctrine that man is a child of God and hence a creature of eternal value and a creature with an eternal destiny. In other words, we reacted with horror and finally with heroism against a way of life which represented Western civilization without Christianity. And we were right, for we saw something entirely different and terrible. The foundation of Western culture, whether we like it or not, is Christian, and we cannot maintain it without believing and practicing that religion.

The most serious thing about our time is not the terrible devastation of the worst war man has known, bad as that is. True, the increase in the destructiveness of modern warfare is serious enough, but there is something that goes beyond that. It is that we have become a generation of word killers. If any man believes that a dead word is no great casualty, let him examine the matter more closely. What happens to a world where such words as justice, truth, love, have either lost their meanings or else been so modified that we can no longer use them when we speak to one another? How can our minds meet or how can we formulate agreements when our vocabularies have no common foundations? All that we have succeeded in building during the past nineteen centuries has been built on these great words. And as long as we were governed by a spirit that kept them alive and kept their definitions clear, we could go on. But if at last we have witnessed the death or deathlike paralysis of the ideas which these words symbolized, then we must start all over again. A civilization rests upon spiritual values whose essence becomes a part of the plain man's life through the words he uses with a common acceptance and a common understanding shared by his fellows.

An illustration of what we are trying to say is to be found in the long-dead tank civilization of Ceylon. Here a great series of tanks and canals was constructed to provide water for the dry plains where the rains never came. The line between the wet and the dry parts of the island is in some places no more than a mile wide. For fifteen hundred years the tank civilization maintained itself in spite of the attack of enemies who always tried to win their victory by destroying the water supply. Finally, the will to rebuild became weaker than the will to destroy and that civilization died. The plains went out of cultivation and the running water became stagnant pools, breeders of malaria. In all probability, if anyone had asked a citizen of that civilization what the foundation of it was, he would have replied that it was the marvelous storage and irrigation system. But he would have been wrong. The real foundation of that civilization was the belief of the people in their way of life that enabled them to withstand their enemies and, when necessary, rebuild what had been destroyed. It does not take very long for the external accomplishments of a culture to be destroyed when the inner faith has gone.

We find ourselves with tremendous powers of communication, but no healing word to speak; tremendous systems of transportation, but nothing to transport that will make life whole again; tremendous powers of production, but no knowledge of how to produce the kind of life that will keep us from committing suicide. We have so little power where we need it most, namely, within our spirits. We have been worshiping for too long that Abomination which makes desolate the inner life of man.

Just before the overthrow of Louis Philippe, Alexis de Tocqueville spoke before the French Chamber of Deputies. He said, "Keep the laws as they are, if you wish. I think that you would be wrong to do so; but keep them. Keep the men too, if it gives you any pleasure. But in God's name change the spirit of your government, for I repeat that spirit will lead you directly to the abyss. . . ." That word could well be spoken to us. It is either a revival of the faith upon which our way of life is built, or it is complete failure. If we still believe that we can be saved by a little more power or more efficient production and cannot salvage time and energy for the consideration of our inner lives where the decision has to be made, we cannot escape an inevitable doom. I am convinced that it is literally true: it is either Christianity or chaos, so far as Western civilization is concerned. The worship of our external accomplishments is the worship of the idol whose gift to his worshipers is death.

Freedom Deified

The popular gospel of our time has been the glorification of freedom and the right of every person to be free. The peculiar thing about it is that the more we talk about it and the more we insist on it as a natural right, the less we experience it. One is reminded of the observation that thousands of women said they would not be dictated to, and then proceeded to become stenographers. Our shrill insistence that we will be free or else, is an indication that we are seeking a substitute for living. It is a sign of the worship of the false god. Once again let it be said that the idol wins its place first of all by promising cheap rewards. Back of all idolatry is the unworthy motive of getting something for nothing. The many sects that try to maintain their connection to Christianity by using its terms, but deny its central truths, all promise that men can have all of its rewards without having to carry the cross. In other words, they can be free. But while they can drug themselves for a time, soon or late life brings them face to face with the fact that they have been under an opiate and not truly alive. What they thought was freedom was actually numbness.

The temple of the idols is thronged by worshipers crying,

"Give to me." The moment the idol demands anything, his temple is deserted. But the living God always puts his divine demands upon men and leads them into the heart of the great paradox, "He that loseth his life, shall find it." For freedom is an empty, neutral term. Freedom for what? Freedom to become what? Freedom to do what? Real Christianity believes that a man must be free to do his duty and to fulfill his obligations. He must be free to fulfill his own destiny. Any other kind of freedom becomes license, which in turn becomes the worst slavery of all.

D. H. Lawrence said it in these words:

> Men are free when they are in a living homeland, not when they are straying and breaking away. Men are free when they are obeying some deep, inward voice of religious belief. Obeying from within. Men are free when they belong to a living, organic, believing community, active in fulfilling some unfulfilled, perhaps unrealized purpose.

It should be noted in passing that if we learn what the responsibilities of freedom are, we will never talk about it so glibly and easily. It is a grievous burden to be born, and, as Mussolini said, men get weary of liberty.

Men are free when they realize they are worth being free. The automaton, or the mere bundle of glands, will never make much sacrifice for freedom because in his heart he knows he is not worth it. It makes very little difference whether such a creature is free or not. The worshiper of the idol is the easiest man to persuade to give up his freedom for a mess of pottage. Only the truly religious man who has been given a vision of himself as a son of God will make the necessary sacrifices for freedom when called upon to do so. When the Abomination of Desolation has been set up, the way is prepared for men to talk much about freedom, and then refuse to accept its responsibilities. The way is also prepared for the coming of the tyrant, and the worship of the state.

All of the nonsense which we have heard talked about a new morality is due to our failure to comprehend the reality of the moral law. We think that morals are just customs and can be changed whenever we so desire. If freedom is deified and we worship it, then why not expect that the god can free us from the tedious demands of morality? But while we are free to choose, we are not free to choose the result of our choosing, as Stanley Jones once said. At last we come to the deep insight of our religion that each man is responsible for all men, and in the service of God alone is to be found perfect freedom. No man understood this better than did the Apostle Paul, who always linked together the idea of being free with the necessity of being a slave of Christ. Religious men are free precisely because they do not prate about their rights, but seek first of all to serve God.

Well, all of this seems a hard saying. But I am convinced that it is the prophetic word of the Gospel to every generation. We are unique in that our time of troubles is more widespread than in other days, and we have more power to do damage to ourselves. But the essential sickness is not unique and at the risk of over-simplification it may be said to be the setting up of the altar of the idol in the temple of God. Whenever that is done, "Those days shall be tribulation," as the Gospel of Mark says. The return to sanity demands that we lose our illusions about our materialistic success, that we become humble, and that we acknowledge our dependence on God. Then if we can become as children, we shall find the method and the direction for our salvation.

In that greatest of all dramatic scenes, the Crucifixion, two thieves were crucified with Jesus. One of them railed on the Galilean and asked to be saved from the cross if Jesus were truly the Son of God. But the other thief rebuked his companion and said that while they were suffering justly, Christ was innocent. "And he said, Jesus, remember me when thou comest in thy kingdom. And he said unto him, Verily

I say unto thee, Today shalt thou be with me in Paradise."
(Luke 23:42–43) Thus one man asked that something be done
to get him out of the trouble he was in, but the other man
asked to be moved into a new environment. We do not need
some specific miracle done for us, but a new center of life and
a new scale of values. This, however, is only possible through
the power released when we worship the true God. Essentially, this is the burden of the prophetic message.

Implications

The Christian preacher ought to be on his guard against
being labeled as one kind of preacher or another. The prophetic strand is one of the most important in the pattern of
his message but it can easily become so prominent that the
pattern loses its symmetry. Especially is this true if the man
is of violent disposition and given to extreme indignations.
He who has the power of vitriolic attack can easily confuse
his own bitterness with his prophetic function.

Many a man was ashamed of himself after the First World
War when he remembered what he had said in the midst of
the conflict. If he was unfortunate enough to have written it
down and had it published, then there was on record a testimony of his loss of temper. His people were in the position
of associating him with their own violence and hatred, for
which they became increasingly ashamed. So in the midst of
some social or political strife, a quick-tempered prophet
may wish in vain that he could recall some hastily spoken
word that was not quite fair and hardly Christian in its
spirit.

The great thing about the Prophets was their ability to
universalize the particular issues. They can speak to us yet
because they were never entangled in a mere local quarrel.
What could so easily have been a few earnest men bickering
with their neighbors came to be great insights into God's
will for justice. The preacher will do well, therefore, to make

sure that he has lifted the local situation into the light of the
eternal principles at stake. When this is done, it is usually
the cure for any personal animosities that might creep in
and color the message.

Perhaps nothing is more important here than the right
motive. If I want to tear open a social situation that smells
to high heaven, let me be sure that it is not because I crave
notoriety, or free publicity. One always comes back to St.
Paul's insight: "If I have not love, it profiteth me nothing."
The model in this respect is Jeremiah, who was hurt by every
bitter word he had to speak, but who went through that
exquisite form of torture because God commanded it. Perhaps it might be said that while we are called to be prophets,
we should be suspicious of ourselves when we come to enjoy
it overly much.

We can sometimes confuse our prophetic calling with dogmatism. The preacher comes to feel that he has been commissioned to tell people what they must do, and to attack
them dogmatically when they will not do it. It is of first
importance to associate ourselves with the people and let
them know we speak to our own sins as well as theirs. Sometimes you will find a man who has so fallen into the habit
of beating the sinners over the heads with hard words that
he has forgotten how to comfort the sinner who repents. To
him, the prophet is a man who knows all the answers and
forces them down people's throats with an utter disregard
for winning men to Christ. We should remember that the
words, "Comfort ye, comfort ye my people, saith your God,"
were spoken by a prophet, and a very great one. The
prophet's word must always come with force, but it can
also come with consideration.

We will do well to be on guard against too much talking
about a favorite sin. Too often it may be merely an effect
rather than a cause. Once again look to the Prophets of the
Old Testament. They went to the root of things and at-

tacked there. We spend too much time bewailing certain social acts which are only revelations of something wrong down much deeper. Men often drink because they are frightened; they steal because they are insecure; they carouse because they have not learned what decent recreation is. Let us not waste our time shouting our imprecations at such as these to the applause of every churchman who never yielded to any of these evils because he was never tempted. But if we are to be true prophets of God, then let us find the causes for such behavior and center our criticism there.

But the most important implication of our prophetic calling is that we are to be men of courage. What an impossible calling is ours if we lack that! The most miserable men I have known are the ministers who are frightened to death lest something they say will offend someone, or something they do will not please someone. We are supposed to have tact and to be governed by a sincere concern for the welfare of our people, but we are not supposed to give a human account for our ministry nor is our chief responsibility to escape criticism.

These are the times that try men's souls indeed, and the Protestant ministry needs to hear a trumpet call to courage in the pulpit. The mouselike message which comes from many a church is a far cry from those spiritual forefathers of ours who threatened to turn the world upside down. It is about time every preacher came to realize that he has a message to proclaim that has the power to knock down every wall of greed and selfish pride. Whether we shall succeed in stemming the headlong rush toward the abyss is not for any man to know. But no generation of preachers ever lived in a situation that so cried aloud for the prophetic message as does this one.

Perhaps someone says that such talk as this is simply a plea for martyrs. I do not think so. It is amazing but it is also true that the vast majority of men expect their preacher to speak his word without fear or favor. They will not always agree, but the fine loyalty of the laymen of the Christian Church is one of those things which makes our profession such a privilege. Only the man who speaks with a sort of conceited dogmatism needs to be concerned about the support of his people. The man who speaks his truth with love and firmness will have the loyalty and support of his people though he may not always have their agreement.

Let us put the whole matter on a very low plane. As I look about at the men who have been called to the large places and who stand out as the commanding voices of their church, I find that they are those who through the years have spoken with frank courage. We have slandered our laymen by our assumption that they wanted merely a milk and water message. They want the Gospel and that includes its prophetic emphasis. Whenever, therefore, our society turns to the worship of the idol, under whatever name or in whatever guise, we are called to denounce it with all the strength we have, and call men back to the worship of God.

IX

TO HEAL THE
BROKEN-HEARTED

> *"He hath sent me to proclaim*
> *release to the captives."*
>
> Luke 4:18

    Preachers need to come back again and again to that dramatic moment in the synagogue at Nazareth when Jesus stood up and read:

> The Spirit of the Lord is upon me,
> Because he anointed me to preach good tiding to the poor:
> He hath sent me to proclaim release to the captives,
> And recovering of sight to the blind,
> To set at liberty them that are bruised,
> To proclaim the acceptable year of the Lord.[1]

There is a sense in which this is the announcement of his platform, or the text of his sermon, or the declaration of his mission. At least so far as Luke is concerned, here is the central meaning of Jesus' work.

    Here in this pronouncement is the great synthesis of what we have called the social gospel, on the one hand, and the personal gospel, on the other. For Jesus the differentiation would have been meaningless and absurd, but for us who are lesser men and the inheritors of a more literal tradition, the problem is a real one. We feel ourselves in conflict between two poles, drawn now this way and now that. Men even have their preaching labeled with the stamp of the social gospel or the personal gospel. That is why it is important to keep our eye on the quotation from Isaiah and remember

---
[1] Luke 4:18–19.

the unity of our message. It will help us to make the necessary combination of our prophetic and our pastoral functions.

Preachers sometimes fall into the pit of separating their social emphasis from the rest of the Gospel. A fine old churchman once remarked, concerning his young preacher, that he thought the world of the young man, but he did wish that he wouldn't take them to task every Sunday morning for Britain's treatment of India. We would not want to intimate that such a subject is not one of importance to every Christian, but after all, what can be done about it is certainly limited, and there is little spiritual food here for daily Christian living.

There is a place for describing social evils which the individual cannot do very much about immediately. But as a steady diet, that kind of preaching becomes harmful because it leads to the conclusion that Christianity has no practical remedies for individual ills. It is like a baby's wail that is often an end in itself. I am convinced that any preacher who has the vision of the whole world in his mind needs to be careful lest he consider the local problem, and the individual distress, beneath his notice. We can become diagnosticians of the cancer at the heart of Western civilization but unable to see or treat the broken heart of the man in the back row.

Perhaps this is more often, though certainly not always, the danger of the young preacher. His favorite text is likely to be "Woe to them that are at ease in Zion," rather than "Come unto me, all ye that labor and are heavy laden." The slashing attack gives more scope for vocal abilities than the ministering unto the spirits wounded in the drab weariness of ordinary living. Besides, the young preacher rightly feels himself more competent to attack social sins than to speak the right word to a suffering man.

Yet most preaching surveys indicate that people feel they are more in need of the personal word. Even young people weary of a constant presentation of general problems and feel a yearning for a flash of light for their own guidance. More times than not, the preacher who is always in hot water over his social interpretations is the man who neglects his pastoral function. With all of our understanding of the broad implications of the Gospel, we should never forget that Christ died for the separate souls of men.

On the other hand, there is the preacher who fairly wallows in individual ethics without ever suggesting or hinting that religion is a matter of social relationships. Too often it happens that the man who goes all out for religious psychiatry comes to the place where he can no longer see a person, but only hidden shames, complexes, and rationalisms. A kind of morbidness takes control of some men, as one semester of abnormal psychology affects some college freshmen. Instead of making them take the sympathetic viewpoint, it affects them with the attitude that there is no health anywhere and if there seems to be, it only means that the person is covering something up.

No preacher who believes in Christianity as a powerful agent in the treatment of sick souls and ailing minds should ever fail to see himself not only as doctor but also as patient. We are individualists, and no group stands under any greater temptation to become one-sided and slightly off balance. A man I knew who was always insisting on treating someone's secret sin always impressed me as being himself in need, not of an amateur but of a professional psychiatrist.

All of this would be unnecessary to think about if we were all of the same stature as our Lord. In him there was blended the perfect understanding of men as units and as social creatures, as unique spirits and as part of a tradition, as alone and in the crowd. But we must think of the Gospel in different categories, though we should always be aware of the arbitrary nature of our division. As the doctrine of the Trinity helps us to consider a part of God at a time, so we must look at and study a part of the Gospel at a time. We have considered the prophetic nature of our message, and now we think of its priestly function as we speak to cure souls.

No one preaches very long without seeing the great need not only for a word of condemnation but for a word of cheer. If the universe is against us, still many a man could maintain his own integrity and courage in the face of that. But when one learns that his real enemy is himself, then the condition is intolerable. In this direction lies suicide, either physical or spiritual. Until the impossible contradictions of our own nature can find some harmony, there is nothing to build on. To the sensitive man in the congregation whose life is one of quiet desperation, we have a word to speak. It is not optimistic in the shallow, popular sense, but it is hopeful.

Hope

The fear of the future is often a glimpse of companionless days which stretch ahead endlessly. There are widows, some of them rich and some of them poor, but all dreaming of a time when there was life about them and they filled a needed place in other lives. There are young couples from small communities trying to find their way in the midst of the large city which is foreign to them and crushes them with a sense of lostness. There is the girl who does not happen to be pretty or stylish, but who has a fine, sensitive nature, waiting for some opportunity to share the wealth of her love. There are the young men who have no money for entertainment and no desire for cheapness in their personal relationships, but who daily become more ready to accept even a sordid relationship rather than have none at all. How many people walk in the darkness of a hopeless loneliness! They have come to what seems an impasse where no decision can be made that is right. They are entangled in their own fears and so hopelessly muddled in their planning that they are ready to do any foolish thing that promises even a temporary relief.

None of us will be foolish enough to assume that loneliness has been vanquished with all of our noise and clever gadgets. Remember the artist who committed suicide and left a note saying that he was tired of inventing devices to get through the twenty-four hours. In every congregation there sits the lonely man, the lonely woman, searching for fellowship and frightened at the look ahead. There are some obvious things like organizations in the church that will serve many of their needs. There ought to be a careful survey of the church program with an attempt to provide a group experience for any person who may not find it anywhere else.

But the preacher has the possibility of ministering unto the lonely directly. One of the great old hymns of the church has it:

> Come ye disconsolate, where'er ye languish,
> Come to the mercy seat, fervently kneel;
> Here bring your wounded hearts, here tell your anguish:
> Earth has no sorrow that heaven cannot heal.
>
> Joy of the desolate, Light of the straying,
> Hope of the penitent, fadeless and pure!
> Here speaks the Comforter, tenderly saying,
> "Earth has no sorrow that heaven cannot cure."
>
> Here see the Bread of Life; see waters flowing
> Forth from the throne of God, pure from above:
> Come to the feast of love; come, ever knowing
> Earth has no sorrow but heaven can remove.
>
> THOMAS MOORE

A part of our message which is too often neglected is the promise of companionship with Christ. It is not always possible to solve the external causes of loneliness, but it is the promise of the Gospel that because loneliness is within,

God meets us there. It is when men are isolated from God and unrelated to His purposes that they become afraid and lose hope. The purposeless drifting and the specter of life as futility are what haunt our solitude with despair. The preacher's word, therefore, is a healing one if it helps to restore faith in God's willingness to dwell with people and walk with them. For at the end of the day it is not solitude in itself that destroys us, but spiritual emptiness which cannot be filled by the crowd.

If life ceases to be an adventure, then there is no substitute for that empty feeling within. The preacher is Christ's trumpet call to join an exciting cavalcade of the saints. It was in this light that a little boy remembered the preaching of his uncle who was a frontier preacher:

> And if Uncle George looked up and said, in tones like big bells, "John, my lad, life is indeed a pilgrimage; we are sojourners, as were our fathers," the boy was not oppressed, but felt intimations of adventure, like a crusader.[2]

This is not to suggest that the solution is either complete or easy, but it is to say that loneliness can be controlled if life means something to us. The preacher is himself a lonely man as long as he maintains his sensitivity, and he should be able to speak the comforting word which is not pity, but duty and heroism.

What the message does is bring light into the fog and darkness and thus remove the uncertainty and worry of the groper. Remember the prayer of Ajax: "O Father Zeus, deliver from the darkness the sons of the Achaeans, make it bright day, permit us to use our eyes; at least destroy us in the sunlight." [3] We do not know all the answers to the questions of suffering men, but we know the Light of the World

---

[2] Beck, "Shadow of a Green Olive Tree," in *Mid-Country*, University of Nebraska, 1945, 160.

[3] *Iliad*, 17, 645.

who gives each man light enough to live by at least a day at a time. Preaching that restores a person's confidence in this will create hope and restore the lonely heart.

But the center of what we must say to those who need hope restored is in the cross. An English chaplain told about a night in 1917 when he stumbled over something in a wood. He stopped to see what it was and saw an undersized, underfed German boy with a wound in his stomach and a hole in his head. And then he saw the boy's face fade away and the Christ on his cross appeared. Said Studdert-Kennedy:

> From that moment on I have never seen the world as anything but a Crucifix. I see the Cross set up in every slum, in every filthy overcrowded quarter, in every vulgar flaring street that speaks of luxury and waste of life. I see Him staring up at me from the pages of the newspaper that tells of a tortured, lost, bewildered world.[4]

Here is the great mystery that out of the worst there comes the best, and shining through the suffering of the Crucifixion there comes the love of God. For it is in this experience that we forget ourselves and remember Him and all our suffering brothers. The word of hope for lonely, discouraged men is in the preaching of the cross. For in some strange way only that can heal the broken-hearted, and give solitude a meaning which makes it bearable and redeeming.

Make-Believe Selves

Among other things, as Mr. Aldous Huxley has said, this is "the age of noise." We are assaulted with unrelated bits of information, and with the development of the radio, even our homes are invaded with noise. The resultant confusion has its influence in all of our lives as it creates a craving for feverish, emotional experiences. Thus do we lose the point of the whole thing and try to live in harmony with some false

---

4 *Religion in Life*, Longmans, Green, 1935, 42.

picture which we have created out of the contemporary madness.

It should not be forgotten that Jesus put his emphasis on helping men to understand their own natures and their own desires. It is noteworthy that he spent so little time talking about what people ought to do, and no time at all in discussing ideals of behavior. He seemed to assume that if men could find the real point of their being—the true picture of themselves—then the main thing in creating balanced living would have been accomplished. So the preacher cannot truly minister to the troubled until he smashes the false selves men accept, and restores the Christian understanding of human nature, its needs and desires.

The preacher will be wrong if he assumes that the well-to-do and the socially successful do not need his healing word. Let him not be so foolish as to think that only the poor and the disinherited are legitimate subjects for his pastoral message. It is true that there are classes of people difficult to reach with a sense of need, at least a sense of the need for religion. But the veneer of their self-sufficiency is often very thin and once you have won their friendship and respect, they will reveal themselves as pitiful in their need. In his *Journal,* Kierkegaard confessed, "I have just returned from a party of which I was the life and soul; wit poured from my lips, everyone laughed and admired me—but I went away . . . and wanted to shoot myself." There are times when our preaching loses its vitality because all unconsciously we assume the role of a chaplain to a group we think never feels despair. We leave the real preaching to the street-corner men and the mission workers.

I have long since lost all my doubts as to the need of all men for the Christian message. And the more successful a man seems to be, the more I feel justified in offering him the opportunity of confessing his fears and seeking the power of God. In this bewildered time you will hardly ever find a person who does not have some urgent inner need. The emptiness of the average man's life is an appalling thing to behold. Preachers need to remember that Christianity was born in the midst of "a failure of nerve" and began its missionary work in an environment of disintegration. Now when the events of our time have evaporated all our self-confidence, we face again the task and the opportunity of calling men to Christ with the promise of faith for living.

I

There are those who have been led to picture themselves as parasites, adhering to something or someone in order to live. Smothered by too much mother love, served by others when they acted helpless, and frightened to death by reality, they have lost their power to stand alone. Through the years they have increased their helplessness and their appeal to sympathy until their own powers are nearly wasted.

There are preachers who depend on winning the pity of their congregations in order to hold their place. There are mothers who maintain the devotion of their families through helplessness and a chronic invalidism which they have manipulated with skill. There are husbands, wives, fathers, who twine about the other members of the household with their demands to be served until they become not living creatures but parasites living on their hosts. For such as these the Gospel has a word which is a sort of divine brutality in that it reveals the shame of the false self and offers the hope of the true self.

These people need to be told that there is no such thing as a natural born hero, or a natural born coward. All men are afraid, but some do not surrender to their fear. What others have done, the poor parasite can learn to do. He can learn to live bravely by living day by day instead of dwelling on the horrible possibilities of the future. The old gentleman who said that he had lived long and had many troubles, most of which had never happened, was speaking for all those who are haunted by fear of the future. In a time when black prophecies are the order of the day, it is encouraging to look back over the past and see how many similar prophecies were false. Jesus' word, "Sufficient unto the day is the evil thereof," is a healing one for the fearful sycophant.

But we are commissioned to tell people that there is One to whom we may cling, who will not let us down. The Prophets were always telling Israel not to put her trust in princes or armies, but in God. For he who stands in the shadow of the Rock will not be deserted. Yet the marvelous thing about it is that the more we lean on God, the more we stand on our own feet, and the more we hold to Him, the more we find personal sufficiency. Men have their dignity restored when their weakness is surrendered to God rather than to one another.

I have not forgotten the simple statement of faith which came to me from a friend who knew little about theological phraseology, but a great deal about the workings of a child-like faith. He said one time that religion to him was like being accompanied by a strong man. On the street corner there waited a bully threatening to beat him. In his fear, my friend was tempted to go around the block or else stay in the house. But the strong man said that they would walk together and he was sure that the situation was not as dangerous as it seemed. But if the bully attacked and more help was needed, my friend could be sure that he would have it. And so life was met each day with confidence because there was always an assurance of more than enough power to fight the battles. We may put it in different terms, but essentially, this is the Gospel's message to the parasite.

II

Then there is the tyrant who has learned that a great many people can be intimidated. He pictures himself as a ruthless leader making others do his will and serve his success. Most organizations know him and sometimes there is one in the home. His blustering spirit is revealed by the words of a man who once said to me half seriously, "Everyone does not like me, but no one ignores me." Yet underneath that man's whole rough exterior there was uncertainty, an empty heart, and a longing for fellowship freely given. Such a one's end is not triumphant, but sordid and sad like a dictator's.

What has the preacher to say to him? He can say that the universe is governed by God, who is love, and that relationships built on force and hatred are fundamentally weak. How cheap seems the blustering of the sons of thunder when compared to the calm strength of Jesus. Thomas Wolfe described a picture of a long line of men extending from the Great Pyramid to the door of Pharaoh's house. There stood the Pharaoh wielding his whip on the back of his chief overseer, who in turn brought his whip down on the man in front of him and thus the process continued until the humblest slave of all felt the lash. But empires as well as lives built on this philosophy are weak.

The Gospel has for the tyrant a new definition of success and a new concept of getting on. To the man who wants to play the part of the grand inquisitor, the word of Christianity comes like the kiss of Christ, to break down the make-believe self and restore a lost humility. This is to set men free from Herod's tragedy, who found it necessary to order that some of the chief men of the city should be slain after his death, for only thus could he be sure there would be mourning in the city. To the tyrant, Christ offers the satisfying relationships of love and service and the assurance of respect and affection.

When Heywood Broun turned to religion, it made quite a stir in the newspapers. After Broun's death, Christopher Morley wrote: "He always took an innocent pleasure in being what used to be known as a Man About Town; and little by little he discovered that the Town that is most interesting is the City of God." So the petty tyrants of life can be introduced to a citizenship based on mutual concern from where their former blustering arrogance seems altogether cheap and pathetic. When Christ's love has cast out his fear, the make-believe tyrant learns how much more interesting and exciting life can be.

III

In every group there is the defeated one who has not found his place in life. Perhaps he is the physically weak person who was never quite up to the ordinary demands of life. He is the socially inept individual who is clumsy and embarrassed in his social relationships. From the defeated experience he tries to salvage some kind of self-esteem by saying, "I don't want that anyway." The man-hater or the woman-hater is often a person who has failed to recover from a defeat or a hurt. In desperation, such people make a virtue of weakness and, fearing that they may be put through another unhappy experience, take refuge in a retreat from life.

For such as these the preacher is entrusted with the word of the great adventure. Christianity inspires each man to recognize his uniqueness and take what he has and make out of that the best he can. The great worth of any man's life is a foundation stone of Jesus' teaching, and we ought to remind people constantly that God counts every hair of our heads. It is an assurance that there is a kind of contribution that can never be made unless we make it. When George Gershwin was invited to be Irving Berlin's secretary, he replied that he was going to write his own songs. The Gospel is a divine encouragement to play our own parts.

Failure is given a different definition from the one given by our success cults. After many failures, Edison's assistant complained that all the work had been done in vain, and Edison replied: "But we have a lot of results; we now know seven hundred things that won't work." Christianity was a great failure according to contemporary standards, and we must remember that it begins not in victory but in defeat. Thus it is able to help men know that the only personal significance in either victory or defeat is the effect the experience has on the person.

Out of this is born courage for the defeated one to try again. If we can help a disappointed man to make one decisive action for Christ's sake, then he can begin the process of his salvation. When Bruce was urged to abandon the attempt to climb Mount Everest in 1924, he replied: "We have left too many of our comrades on the heights to abandon the road." A new lonely kind of courage comes to the frightened as they are led into the fellowship of the saints who have gone on before. Failure becomes not a source of shame but a cause for gladness that we have had a part in the great contest.

There keeps coming back to me the picture of two men who stand in such complete contradiction to each other that they illustrate sharply this thing we are considering. One of them is what the world calls a successful man. He is successful financially, socially, and morally. But he is the most timid man I've ever known in some ways, for he never speaks or acts without making sure that his success will not be jeopardized. Life to him is a matter of never meddling with what does not concern him directly, and thus when one comes to know him, he is a man who walks a careful, fearful way.

The other man is always on the losing side. He attacks social situations without considering the cost to himself personally, if he has a chance to strike even a feeble blow for the disinherited. He never seems to be much concerned about whether he can win or not, but on the other hand, there is a quality in him that makes him impervious to defeat. I cannot help but feel that at the end of the day, to call the first man successful and the second man a failure is all wrong.

For when one knows the inner life of each man, the first has built on the sand, and the latter on the rock. The Gospel is the birth of courage because it calls men to march to a different music, and judge their results by a different standard.

IV

We will be preaching to the proud whose vision of themselves is seen through the dark glass of their egos. They must be first in every undertaking and they have never learned the joy of humility because they have never been able to seek the forgiveness of their sins. They are dependent on the good will of the majority and will compromise a principle or a friend if by so doing they can win applause. In them there is no depth and no integrity.

Now Christianity does not cure pride by reducing life to a dead level. It believes in the distinction of worth. Whenever we are talking about the saints, we are talking about a kind of superiority that shames the boisterous vulgarity of egocentric pride. If we can learn to portray the quiet nobility of the person who has surrendered his pride to God in contrast to the pitiful Neros of our society, our preaching will have a healing touch.

One of the loveliest persons I ever knew stopped one day for a conference. She had come from the doctor, who had told her frankly that she had a few months, perhaps a few weeks, to live. But that was not what troubled her. She wanted to know if I thought it best to tell her family and friends, or to keep it from them. Which would cause them the least pain in the end and be the kindest thing to do? And when I thought of her and compared that spirit with those who feverishly trample over their brethren to snatch what they call success, I felt that if I could make my people feel what I felt, there would be a change in all of our measurements of success. Remember how John Bunyan in his

Pilgrim's Progress made this so plain when he wrote of Mr. Valiant-For-Truth's passing: "So he passed over and all the trumpets sounded for him on the other side."

How easily St. Paul could have been a self-centered star if he had not been captured by Christ. If John Wesley had not been under the compulsion of the spirit of his Lord, how selfishly dictatorial he might have been. If there sits in the congregation a man who is consumed by his own pride and a hunger for applause, we have a word which can destroy his selfish make-believe self, salvage all of his good ability, and direct it toward a real triumph.

To Feel Important

The minister whose relations are not confined to a particular class soon learns that the world is full of people who never receive recognition or appreciation. When a man once asked Lord Curzon if he was anybody in particular, he no doubt did more to deflate him than if he had defeated him in a contest. For each man wants to be somebody in particular. Even a dog can be made miserable by being ignored or treated harshly. When we refuse service in a restaurant to any man, we are heaping upon him the chief indignity, for we are treating him as if he were not important enough to be fed.

There are those who interpret Christianity as a philosophy of negation. Nietzsche was in this tradition when he talked about a "slave-morality." Too often a kind of conscious unselfishness is encouraged which pays honor to the person who goes about in a nosy sort of way, doing good unto others. As someone once pointed out, you can tell who the others are by the hunted look on their faces. Or we grovel in humiliating expressions and sing lustily about being a worm. Professional religious workers sometimes become slovenly and incompetent in their work all in the name of giving up personal ambition.

The Gospel is not rightly understood when it becomes this kind of teaching. The unselfishness it teaches is not something to make others unhappy when it is present, but a self-forgetfulness which brings joy. Men are not worms, but creatures made a little lower than the angels, and potential sons of God and brothers of Christ. I have known a few preachers who boasted of their lack of ambition but I never felt they did the Kingdom of God much service. Our faith does not come to silence the desire to be important, but to teach men how to be important legitimately. It is, in a word, to rescue men from mediocrity, to take them out of the crowd and crown them with the glory of their calling. Men who have heard the Word truly preached will not slink away but will walk a little straighter, with more assurance of their value.

This is not done by making men feel that they are protected but by making them feel that they are needed. We need to be needed, for only then are we sure of our importance. There is no better illustration of that than Tamsen Donner, who although not too strong, weathered that horrible winter in the Sierras while strong men weakened and died. I think the source of her strength was the needs of her husband and her children, which called forth strength and endurance she never knew she possessed. When anyone needs me, he has ministered unto me, for I am never so sure of my personal significance as when he asks for my help.

Horrible as war is, it fulfills an important function in a society that allows great numbers of its citizens to believe there is no place for them. For in time of war, everyone is needed whether he is young or old, rich or poor, strong or weak. William James spoke about the necessity of finding a moral equivalent for war, and nowhere is the truth of his observation more apparent than here. Men will give their ultimate devotion to sheer brutality rather than pay lip service to an ideal that merely tolerates them and has no real place for them.

The Christian faith is a trumpet call to battle, to struggle, to heroism. The preacher must rescue every man from his sense of unimportance by sounding Christ's call to service and enlisting each man's life in the crusade for righteousness. Let the Church be the Church, but let it never forget that it is involved in society and it must be relevant to our industrial civilization. We will be wrong if we assume that because we cannot realize the Kingdom of God through legislation, we are absolved from all further duty except prayer. The Gospel rescues men from their inferiority by making them soldiers in the social struggle for righteousness and justice.

We can make men feel important if they are encouraged to stand for something bigger than themselves and something that will remain when they are gone. The Church is the communion of saints and it ennobles each member. What preacher does not feel that while he may not be so important in himself, he is a symbol of his church and that is very important. Any man's life is made great or small in accordance with the things he stands for and the purposes he strives to realize. If we can succeed in giving a person something bigger than he is to which he can give his final loyalty, we have ministered unto his weak spirit. "For to me to live is Christ," said Paul, and in that he found the legitimate satisfaction for his desire to excel.

The healing power of the Gospel is great because men must be healed within themselves. A brilliant marriage does not necessarily make men feel important. One psychologist remarked that half of his patients were neurotic because they were married and half were neurotic because they were not. It is trite to say that money does not do it. Certainly one more scholastic degree will not work the miracle. Finally we learn that only as men are strong within, through their faith in a purpose for themselves and all men, are they aware of their own place in the eternal scheme of things.

To have an adequate faith gives confidence and the sense of well-being. The old Negro's prayer is to the point: "Lord, help me to know that there ain't nothing going to happen to me that you and I together can't take care of." Any man who is honest knows that there is no guarantee that he will be a hero in any given situation. But the Christian finds his assurance in his dependence on the power of God. It is this adequacy that brings confidence.

I agree with Clifton Fadiman that to read about dreams is not interesting. I relate my most common nightmare, therefore, only as a revealing phenomenon. I am always standing before a large crowd that has come to hear me speak, but suddenly, I know I have nothing to say. Something has interfered with my preparation and in that horrible moment I must sit down in confusion and disgrace. It is a great relief to awaken, for few experiences are more terrible than an experience of inadequacy. But as preachers, we are sent to speak a word which rescues every man from insignificance and inadequacy. For the Gospel makes every man feel important.

To Find One's Life

Perhaps the majority of the frustrated, unhappy people of the world are victims of an inability to forget themselves. They have listened to the so-called charm school psychology, which advises that to recover self-confidence, one should look at oneself in the mirror and softly murmur one's own name. This, in the case of most people, is precisely the thing they should not do. How different is Jesus' treatment of the broken-hearted. He teaches men to pray by centering their thoughts on God and their brethren. He insists that only as men lose their lives can they find them. He drives self-pity out by helping men catch a vision of the suffering world and its needs. The preacher's healing ministry will never be successful on any other basis than his Lord's.

We become sick when we lose our sense of wonder and awe. In one of Strindberg's plays a man inquires about the health of another man's wife and is told that she is almost blind. "That is too bad," says the man, but the other replies: "No, she says there is nothing worth seeing and she hopes she will soon be deaf because there is nothing worth hearing, and she says the best thing about being old, is that you are almost through." This is an extreme case, but disillusionment and cynicism are a part of that same spirit. How different are children! Kenneth Grahame said that he wrote about children and animals because "the most priceless possession of the human race is the wonder of the world." Men need to be rescued from an arrogant materialism that assumes all wonder can be put into a test tube. The Gospel has a childlike quality about it which restores freshness to the jaded, weary spirits of men. To present that is to restore our ability to worship and to re-establish our humanity.

Misapprehensions and misunderstandings are possible only where there is no love. We cannot truly understand ourselves and our desires until we learn to love. The world reveals itself only partially, and even then with distortion, to the man who is bitter and has no charity. The Gospel's message of love and forgiveness not only heals the broken heart but also makes whole the broken mind and the distorted vision. We find our life through love.

Thus our message becomes one of healing the broken-hearted, restoring confidence to the fearful, making each man feel important, and proclaiming how man may find life. We preach a sense of mission "that it may not be through our surrender that the great experiment of existence, whose issue remains in doubt, come to an end in nothingness." [5]

---

[5] Dixon, *The Human Situation,* Longmans, Green, 1935, 438.

Thus is Christ able to rescue every generation from its frustrations and its futilities.

Implications

If we have been called to speak the word which can heal the broken-hearted, our mood must be one of assurance. The fumbling, almost apologetic manner of some men in the pulpit speaks louder to the seeker in the pew than words. If our manner does not proclaim that the Gospel has worked for us, we can hardly hope to convince another man that it will work for him. The person who needs to hear the promise of the Great Physician and needs to believe that there is an answer to his suffering, will not find his needs fulfilled by negatives. It is a sad thing to leave a service without being conscious of how positive a thing is Christianity and what miraculous things it can do to broken lives.

It goes back, I suppose, to whether or not we have a real concern for men, and whether we have a real confidence in the efficacy of the Gospel. One layman remarked that he would never go to his pastor for real help because he would feel that he was talking to an orator but not to a pastor. The healing of Jesus sprang from his sympathy and love for each person. The preacher must feel this so deeply that in his spoken message men will see shine through the spirit of the Good Samaritan, who was not too concerned with his own journey and his own plans to stop and minister to the wounded. I cannot help but feel that it will be done best by the man who himself has been on the edge of the abyss and found his salvation in Christ.

It is here that a man's message is so dependent on his pastoral function. I went to a wrestling match once, and I have wondered ever since why people go more than once. The man who took me said that he thought it was good for a preacher to see real life now and then. I remembered some of my pastoral experiences during the past days. I had conducted a funeral service and tried to comfort a young mother and two children who had been left without means of support. I had talked with a young man who had been drunk for a week trying to forget a girl he had been living with, and who had finally deserted him. I had counseled with a broken-hearted young woman whose husband wanted a divorce. I recalled the old lady with no money, no friends, no family, who had to be helped to find courage for the closing chapter of her life. There was the fifteen-year-old boy whose stepfather had developed an antipathy to him that made his home life unbearable. The Christian pastor sees more real life, when his people come to trust him, than he will see at a wrestling match if he attends every night in the year.

I have found it helpful to headline in my pastoral prayer some broken heart in my parish. In this very difficult part of the worship service, we will find difficulty in lifting our congregation to God by using generalities. If I can pray for some particular man or woman (not by name, of course) and let his or her situation fill my mind as I pray, the prayer will come closer to ministering to the needs of all the congregation. If a man's mind is filled with his pastoral experiences, his prayers will be safeguarded against becoming a flowery list of petitions which no one really expects to be answered because they do not have the needs of particular men in them. Nor will they have a monotonous sameness about them which is so often apparent, even in the preacher's heroic struggle for variety.

What has been said about the prayer is also applicable to the sermon. When men preach with definite human tragedies before them, there is added to their message the power of a new urgency. The preacher does not need to be embarrassingly personal to let people know that he has firsthand knowledge of that which he speaks. Ultimately, this part of his preaching will depend on his worthiness to be to his people as the shadow of a great rock in a weary land.

Hans Zinsser wrote describing an experience that deeply influenced his attitude toward his profession:

> I remember one dark, rainy day when we buried a Russian doctor. A ragged band of Serbian reservists stood in the mud and played the Russian and Serbian anthems out of tune. The horses on the truck slipped as it was being loaded, and the coffin fell off. When the chanting procession finally disappeared over the hill, I was glad that the rain on my face obscured the tears that I could not hold back. I felt in my heart, then, that I never could or would be an observer, and that, whatever Fate had in store for me, I would always wish to be in the ranks, however humbly or obscurely; and it came upon me suddenly that I was profoundly happy in my profession, in which I would never aspire to administrative power or prominence so long as I could remain close, heart and hands, to the problems of disease.

So the preacher needs to know that there is no higher position for him than to keep close to the spiritual and mental diseases of people and minister to them in the name of the Great Physician.

The closer the delivery of the sermon is to private conversation, the better. A pompous pulpit tone cannot minister to the broken-hearted, nor can the man who gives the impression of anonymity in his speaking. The direct word from a particular man to a particular man concerning a particular problem or state of mind is the kind of speech that finds its goal.

This means that the sermon must arrive at an answer. Too much preaching spends its time in analyzing what is wrong when all of that is already obvious. But what has Christianity to offer in the way of solution? What definite steps can a man take in order to reach the goal of meaningful living? Let us not despise techniques of prayer, or directions of how to develop new habits for old. It is here that psychology can serve us, and the way men seek help in learning how to win friends and influence people ought to indicate that our preaching is in vain if we do not help them with practical directions.

This does not mean that we must always know the details of how a man can solve his personal problems. It does mean that we must not leave vague sentimental longings hanging in the air. Men should leave church with one or two definite things they can do, if they will, to find life. Perhaps the best sign of effective preaching is the number of calls the preacher has for personal counseling. That means that he has succeeded in restoring hope and arousing confidence in Christianity as healing. The details can only be worked out in private conversation, but the faith that it is worth while trying Christ must be created through the sermon. Robert Frost said to a class, "I am not a teacher, but an awakener." The preacher is not always a solver of problems, but he ought to be an awakener of confidence in God. If we believe and preach that God can and will provide for any man's life a new center, a new purpose, and a new service, our preaching will be redemptive. To a fate-worshiping generation caught in the clutches of inexorable law, it is a great thing to be able to proclaim: "Behold, I make all things new."

In John Masefield's *Everlasting Mercy,* Saul Kane leaned out of the window in a revulsion against his companions and felt blowing through the market place a cool wind that touched his face like grace. To the broken-hearted, enflamed with the fever of their worry, their sin, their hopelessness, the preacher needs to be as the cooling wind of God's grace. His office is not the miraculous wiping out of the past or the waving of a wand which will break the fetters of the present. But it is to re-establish a broken relationship with a God who cares enough to walk the hard road back to wholeness with any person who will truly repent. The preacher is empowered to present a message with such wondrous promise that every needy man begins to feel that there is healing in the Gospel for him.

X

POWER TO THE FAINT

*"Even the youths shall faint
and be weary."*

Isaiah 40:30

If it were not so tragic, it would be a source of grim amusement to note that in the very time our search for power has been so amply rewarded, we are more frightened and less competent in controlling life than ever before. A materialistic philosophy has taught that our chief troubles were lack of goods and comforts. If only we could produce enough to eat, enough to wear, and housing, then according to this viewpoint the chief obstacles in the way of establishing utopia would have been eliminated. Back of the development of what some have called *scientism* there has been the underlying assumption that our real problems are physical, and once we have learned to control the physical universe, we will have no further difficulties.

There were a few men who doubted this belief and pointed out that instead of solving all our problems, the development of power would create new and greater ones. Here and there men held to the religious idea that, because of his nature, man would always find himself the chief problem. Tolstoy said, "If the arrangement of society is bad (as ours is), and a small number of people have power over the majority and oppress it, every victory over nature will inevitably serve only to increase that power and that oppression. This is what is actually happening." [1] Certainly we

---

1 Quoted by Huxley, *Science, Liberty and Peace*, Harper, 1946.

have discovered that if human relations are wrong, then the increase of power simply makes them worse.

Too much power dwarfs men and makes them victims instead of masters. Henry Adams saw this possibility before it had developed to the present crisis, and he wrote: "Modern politics is, at bottom, a struggle not of men but of forces. The men become every year more and more creatures of force, massed about central powerhouses. The conflict is no longer between the men, but between the motors that drive the men, and the men tend to succumb to their own motive force." [2] Increasingly it becomes clear that men do not have power but power has men. In our understanding of the nature of power and the nature of men, we have been too naïve and we awaken to this truth when it is almost too late.

If this factor is still unappreciated by the men on the street, certainly it is all too clear to the atomic scientists. In fact it has become so clear that these have deserted their historic objectivity and mounted the pulpit to warn of imminent danger unless men find moral power to control atomic power. They know and they try to warn us that things are out of hand and that our very existence is a matter of touch and go.

The Failure of Power

For a background of our danger, we need to recognize that in the minds of many people Christianity is a failure and, hence, the West needs a new basis for its life. They do not always say it openly, but underneath the surface there has been a good deal of murmuring against Christianity's failure to prevent war or to appeal to the majority of successful men as a way of life. This feeling found its embodiment in the

---

2 Adams, *The Education of Henry Adams*, Random House, 1931.

Nazi experiment, which substituted power for Christ as the foundation of its philosophy.

That controlled experiment in Germany lasted long enough for us to draw certain conclusions from it. Here was a denial not only of Christian practice, which is common enough in all places, but of Christian theory. Our inherited ethical ideas lost their meanings because they were Christian concepts which no longer were admitted as real. In their place was put an accent on sheer power, on leadership, and on authority. Science, the universities, the churches, found they could not exist any longer as seekers after truth. They existed as slaves of a master-race concept, and were tolerated only as a means to an end.

That experiment failed militarily, and according to Nazism's own criterion, that was final, for it had said that if a thing could not defend itself, it ought to go down. But it failed also in living up to its promises as the basis of a new order. The direction it took showed that it would never be able to produce a new civilization but, on the contrary, would establish a world gangsterism, and lead man backwards to savagery. We know now that civilization is not possible on the basis of power alone, for power is self-destructive.

This is indeed a serious situation, for so many of the deluded have nothing to put in its place. There is a great emptiness in our life which will be filled with seven devils worse than the one driven out unless we find faith. Outwardly we are still intact, but when one penetrates the outer walls, he is appalled to see nothing but a shell. In 1918 when General Haig ordered attacks against the strong German fortifications south of Bayaume, he said to Churchill: "Now you will see what these fortifications are worth when troops are no longer resolved to defend them." Even so, a society has no defense if it is manned by "troops no longer resolved," because they no longer believe.

We have been adequate when it came to facing particular

enemies if it was a matter of massing great power against them. But in this serious tribulation which has fallen upon us, that is not enough because it is not to the point. Now it is a demand for wisdom and control that we face in the long pull ahead. Patience, never a popular virtue, is called for if our efforts are to result in peace. The Duke of Wellington, in explaining some British victories over the French, said that British soldiers were not braver than French soldiers, they were only brave five minutes longer. But that staying power is produced by a great sense of destiny, which in turn is born out of a vision of eternity. Men discover that mere cleverness is no substitute for spiritual control.

Now concerning all of this there is a large amount of agreement. There is not much enthusiasm when some personal sacrifice has to be made in order to find a new basis for life, but theoretically, at least, not many people believe that all is well. Yet it is not so easy to pick up the broken pieces and begin to build again. You cannot say, "We need faith, therefore we will produce faith." The cry is for a new marching song, but like another group of exiles we can only lament: "How shall we sing the Lord's song in a strange land?" We cannot bring ourselves to make the radical readjustments which we will have to make if we are to recover from our terror.

The Answer

We must come to a realization that religion is a very powerful affair, in spite of modern man's doubt, and that what stands in our way even as we celebrate military victory, is a number of bad religions. We fought against one of them but you cannot annihilate religion by force or argument, or education. The only way to defeat an evil religion is to replace it with a good one. It will be true, finally, that men will march for something and they will believe passionately, for good or ill. Our future, therefore, depends on whether or not there is a religion that can control science by affecting character.

To put this in another way, we must now do something about human nature. If it is true that nothing can ever be done here and human nature does not change, then there is no word of hope to speak. For men must be lifted to a level above the demagogue's influence. They must become mature enough to be unmoved by militarists who still prate about safety by way of threats based on huge military establishments. In a situation that reveals insanity in the minds of many leaders, and when even the irreligious begin to speak of sin, man must be saved.

We stand at a moment such as faced the Disciples when they had heard Jesus' hard word concerning the difficulties of the rich getting into the Kingdom of God. "Who then can be saved?" they asked. Jesus replied, "With men this is impossible; but with God all things are possible." [3] The problem is a religious one and the answer will be a religious answer. This is to say that in God alone can we hope to find the solution to our power dilemma. A religion that can release constructive power is the only basis of hope.

The Christian Doctrine

Christianity goes always to the root of the problem in that it goes to the nature of God and the nature of man. Just now it is especially important that we should understand man's nature. Back of all social, political, and economic thought there is an assumption about man. He is thought to be either good or bad, rational or emotional, slave or freeman. The main reason for the failure of our power culture is its misunderstanding of human nature. We can never do the hard and painful task of patching the old world or

---

[3] Matthew 19:26.

building a new one until we have examined ourselves and decided what kind of creatures we are.

Nor is there any sense in talking about our rights as human beings until we know something of what we are capable of being. Democracy is always tempted to stress the rights of man and ignore the nature of man. Fascism is in just as great error on the side of obligations, for even the discussion of the duties of man rests upon a more ultimate question. Carlyle's remark concerning the French Constitution of 1789 is always relevant:

> With endless debating we get the *Rights of Man* written down and promulgated: true paper basis of all paper constitutions. Neglecting, cry the opponents, to declare the *Duties of Man*! Forgetting, answer we, to ascertain the *Mights of Man;* one of the fatalist omissions.[4]

This fatal omission has been brought to our attention in these days by the failure of a shallow liberalism whose faith in the goodness and power of man to realize his goodness has been relegated to the same shelf with the "glad girl" stories. We may be in danger of going to the other extreme and subscribing to a pious fatalism which places all power in the hands of a transcendent Deity, leaving man quite helpless to do anything for the salvation of his world. We need to redefine the Christian understanding of human nature.

There are several reasons for turning back to St. Paul for an exposition of the Christian doctrine of man. In spite of the fact that he puts his thought into abrupt and extreme forms and often uses a vocabulary that seems strange to us as well as exaggerated, no man understood better the real implications of that religious movement which began with Jesus. He is the supreme example of a man defeated and filled with despair because of the insoluble contradictions

---

4 Carlyle, *French Revolution*, I, Bk. VI, Ch. 2.

within his own nature, who found harmony through a religious experience within Christianity. He is the man who found the source of power for the conquest of an empire. His own interpretation of that experience has had what might be termed a "normative" influence on our faith. The Christian doctrine of man has been, broadly speaking, based on the seventh chapter of Romans. There has been effective power in his psychology as well as in his theology, and the Church is always turning back to it. The greatness of Augustine and Luther lies chiefly in the fact that they rediscovered Paul during critical periods in the Church's history. Nearly every great revival of Christianity has been, among other things, a rediscovery of Paul. It is hardly too much to say that when Christianity has been most powerful, it has been, generally speaking, the Christianity of St. Paul.

The Apostle puts his thought into two main categories. First of all, he speaks of "the natural man," and secondly, he speaks of "the spiritual man." Out of this contrast there has grown the impression that Paul is speaking of the dualism associated with Greek philosophy. It must be conceded that many Christians have interpreted Paul so that the spiritual is good and the flesh is evil. Moderns have too often blamed Paul for this unhealthy dualism. But a careful study of the Pauline letters will correct this misinterpretation.

The natural man is not necessarily a depraved man at all, and the doctrine of natural depravity did not begin with Paul. He believes too much in men and he is too willing to insist on moral standards for all mankind to make depravity a possible doctrine in his theology. The natural man may believe in Judaism and hold to its pure monotheism and high ethical consciousness, or he may be a sincere worshiper of the pagan gods. He may even recognize God's divine demands and his own obligation to fulfill them. Such people are all about us. They are the ones who want ethics without religion and strive to find a basis for ethical behavior apart from God. Paul was very pessimistic about men apart from Christ because he saw them as living on borrowed insights and lacking an adequate dynamic.

The natural man is one whose duties are painful and unpleasant. The joy of religion is not present, and while the moral code is still recognized, it exercises only a negative fascination. The small boy who was theatened with the displeasure of Santa Claus or God whenever he was bad said with exasperation, "If it were not for Santa Claus or God, I could have some fun." So natural men are often to a greater or lesser degree like that, or like materialists who see a natural, gay, pagan world made drab by Jesus. Because of his own inner uncertainty, the natural man finds relief by blaming religion's emphasis on moral duties.

The natural man, therefore, is hopelessly dualistic, for he is aware of two natures struggling within him. Novelists have given this conflict its popular expression, and psychologists have their classical cases of split personalities. Paul gave one of the clearest descriptions of a man aware of his disintegrated, warring self when he wrote:

> For the good which I would I do not: but the evil which I would not, that I practise. But if what I would not, that I do, it is no more I that do it, but sin which dwelleth in me. I find then the law, that, to me who would do good, evil is present. . . . O wretched man that I am! who shall deliver me out of the body of this death? [5]

The natural man, therefore, is in a state of powerlessness. Life is not safe for him, and in the face of evils which he deplores there seems no way to control it. The world is too much for him, and though he seeks to put on a good front and to keep a calm appearance, down below the surface there is stark, indecent fear. Tomorrow is a nightmare and his life moves in the direction of failure with the inevitability

---

[5] Romans 7:19–21, 24.

of a Greek tragedy. All of this is much worse because it must
be hidden and kept secret. One must pretend that all is well
and mouth the slogans that now have a grim mockery about
them. To confess the secret terror would only enlarge the
hole in the dam and let the deluge in that much sooner.
In the very hour that the natural man threatens loudest and
boasts of his materialistic power, the hand writes on the wall.

But Paul found his solution when Jesus met him on the
Damascus Road and turned his face in another direction.
To him, the change seemed as great as coming from death
into life. Perhaps it is in his description of the change that
the influence of his Greek environment is most apparent. It
was not a gradual growth from the natural man into the
spiritual man, but a catastrophic upheaval. It was like being
crucified and rising again; it was, in a word, the kind of
experience that might come to a tempestuous genius. We
should be grateful that in describing the experience, Paul
used such clear, sharp terms that we cannot miss his meaning. Even if the experience does not come to us with the
same shattering impact, Paul helps us to understand the
meaning of what Christ does for weak humanity.

Human nature touched by Christ begins to produce the
fruits of the Spirit, which are, among other things, "love,
joy, peace." This is not to say that we are saved from sorrow
or failure, but that we find the deep happiness of those who
have overcome the world. It is the kind of life that makes a
man like Paul break through bitter controversy, unjustified
criticism, and sickness, with a burst of praise or a poem on
love. There is such power in this joy that the biologist Ro-
manes became a believer when he observed how it is created
by Christianity.

The spiritual man is an integrated personality whose
struggles are no longer meaningless and self-contradictory.
Life makes sense to him, and the quality of his character
becomes the most convincing testimony that there is mean-

ing at the center of things. The universe is no longer a chaos to the spiritual man, and even nature produces a chord out of the silence. Job speaks of it as a time

> When the morning stars sang together,
> And all the sons of God shouted for joy.[6]

To the natural man nature is only murder, cruelty, and bloodshed. It is as if the physical world can be little more than a reflection of a man's own inner being. Certainly nature does not groan for redemption until a man can see it as did the Apostle Paul. To him, the world belonged to God, whose will it was to bring all things into harmony with Himself. The ultimate factor, therefore, in describing the meaning of nature, is not the facts observed but the quality of the spiritual life of the observer.

A man like Admiral Byrd catches something of the rhythm of the universe as he observes a dying day while keeping his long vigil at the South Pole. A poet like Wordsworth feels it in every passing cloud and every field of flowers. For most of us, especially if we are city dwellers, all of this passes us by. One of the serious things that happens to an urban civilization is its loss of oneness with all the created world of God. Part of the fragmentariness of our personal lives is due to this, and men have difficulty maintaining their sense of wholeness. The spiritual man is not a pantheist, but out of the unity of his own inner life he sees a unity of all things in God.

Mysticism, I suppose, has something to do with this sense of unity. John Wesley looked with suspicion upon the mystics, which suspicion, incidentally, I share. Yet the mystic who loses himself in the ocean of God's being is a witness to this true experience of wholeness which the spiritual man knows. But there is a vast difference between being lost in an ocean and being aware of a Person whose will gives every-

---

[6] Job 38:7.

thing a meaning beyond itself. There can never be any doubt that the God who meets us in Jesus respects each person and He has no desire to engulf any man in an atmosphere that melts the distinct boundaries of his personality. The spiritual man has the consciousness of God's standing over against him, and in no way overriding him. It is the experience of belonging to God and His world by virtue of a free choice which is never the surrender of one's personal integrity.

This sense of belonging comes to men who find at the heart of things the God who meets them in Christ. That relationship cuts straight through all the conflicts, the unanswered longings, the inadequacy. The testimony of the saints is the antidote for the cultural pessimism that follows all materialistic philosophy. Man is God's creature and not the slave of his fellows, his time, or himself. This is the new fellowship, the new reconciliation, the new power which springs from the experience described by Paul.

The power of the Christian is the power of weakness, and it is this paradoxical nature of it that makes us unwilling to accept it. Man comes to harm when he knows he is weak but thinks that perhaps he can become strong through his own strength. A great deal of imperialism has been developed under the philosophy of the white man's burden, by which we have justified our rule of "native" populations for our own advantage. But once we seek to compensate for our weakness on our own terms, then we become the worst of all possible sinners. It is hard for modern men to believe that men are strong not when they tyrannize over others but when they fall upon their faces and confess: "I am a man of unclean life"; or with eyes downcast they pray: "God be merciful to me a sinner"; or when like Peter they fall at the feet of Jesus and say: "Depart from me, Lord, for I am a sinful man."

There are too many great men in the world who put themselves above mankind to rule it. There are too many legislators and organizers who want to manipulate people, for the people's own good of course. Power comes only when we can identify ourselves with people as common creatures in need. Human pride is the great barrier to the power of God.

The spiritual man has found power to live by nobly, heroically, joyously. Professor Sperry wrote:

> Liberal Protestantism is out of touch with the whole Pauline conception of the Christian life, not because it cannot translate Paul's rabbinical ways of thought but for a far deeper reason. It is not accustomed to think of the initial commitments of the Christian life as above all else the quest for power, the power which saves us from ourselves and from the world, and makes us, out of weakness, strong.[7]

There is a sense in which the spiritual man of power cannot be born until the natural man has looked into the horror of seeing nothing beyond himself. It is out of that critical situation that a man learns humility, without which his quest for power is in vain.

The man who seeks power as an end in itself is foredoomed to failure. Bertrand Russell believed that the four men who had more power than any others were Buddha and Christ, Pythagoras and Galileo. Yet as he points out, none of these had political support and none was regarded as successful in his own lifetime. But the important observation is in these words: "No one of the four would have affected human life as he has done if power had been his *primary* object." Like happiness, it comes as a by-product of other things, and the power which God gives to the faint comes when, asking for no selfish gift, we wait upon the Lord.

Nature of Ethics

One of the distressing things about modern man is not his relatively high ethical consciousness but his powerless-

---

[7] Sperry, *Reality in Worship,* Macmillan, 1925.

ness in the face of crude emotional movements. Civilization
stands like a group of nice elderly gentlemen of the old
school, waiting helplessly the attack of the next gang of
hoodlums who neither know nor respect the rules of the
game. It stands like a brave picket willing to hold its post to
the end, but knowing that the final outcome is no longer in
doubt. How easy it is for a small group to provoke a crisis
that threatens the whole civilized experiment. How empty
of purpose and power are all the well-meaning people who
vaguely hope against hope that we can muddle through.

We have misunderstood the nature of ethics, and we have
assumed that they are cause instead of result. If we repeat
the words, we have assumed that the will of men would
respond. It is not so, and, in fact, the truth is just the contrary. Ethics are a result of religion and they cannot stand
on their own feet. Elton Trueblood's penetrating phrase,
"a cut-flower civilization," describes a way of life that has
divorced itself from its faith and hoped that the ethics of
that faith would continue to maintain themselves. You may
say practice the Golden Rule, or love your enemies, or sacrifice for the common welfare, but if anyone asks the secularist
why, the whole business collapses. It collapses unless you
can reply it is God's will that men should so behave, and
that Christ died to show God's deep concern for each man.
That is to say, if there is no religious answer to give, there
is no real answer at all.

Men act the way they believe, and they believe with their
hearts. No intellectual set of principles has power enough
to influence deeply the behavior of men. Ethics without a
religion are never a match for even an immature religion
without ethics. It is religion that is powerful, and the bad
religions will continue to dominate men if their only rivals
are codes of ethics. Our only hope is to set loose against them
the Gospel of Christ, which "is the power of God unto salvation to every one that believeth." Alexander Cowie said that

modern novelists lacked the power of the older ones because of their lack of personal concern for men. But you cannot care enough unless you can look through the eyes of Christ. Jesus not only preached ethics—the Stoics did that—but he released God's power to men.

Among the personal effects of a serviceman killed in the South Pacific there was a notebook in which he had written:

> This is the time for a new revelation. People don't think much about religion nowadays. But we need a voice from on High, brother, and I don't mean maybe. This thing has got out of human ability to run. I'm no religious fanatic. But we are in a situation where something better than human brains has got to give us advice.

What this boy felt was what all men must discover soon or late. To keep our world from being a madhouse, we must find a power not ourselves that will make for righteousness. Ethics are helpless; only a vital Christianity can save us from ourselves.

Implications

It is about time that Christianity's inferiority complex should be healed. If there was ever a time when the realism of our faith is apparent, and when Christian preachers should be aware of the need for something which only they can supply, that time is the twentieth century. We are purveyors of power. Against the crumbling, deteriorating defenses of Western culture, we can proclaim that "a mighty fortress is our God." It was summed up in the classic statement by Isaiah:

> He giveth power to the faint; and to him that hath no might he increaseth strength. Even the youths shall faint and be weary, and the young men shall utterly fall: but they that wait for Jehovah shall renew their strength; they shall mount up with wings as eagles; they shall run, and not be weary; they shall walk, and not faint.[8]

---

[8] Isaiah 40:29–31.

Too much preaching is a fevered appeal to lift oneself by
sheer determination. Too many times a man leaves a service
with the impression that religion is an added burden one
agrees to carry. Our good news is that there is something to
carry us, and it will make even the difficulties of this mortal
life a source of joy. That always seems a little absurd to the
worldling. But to men who have found life too much for
them and are fearful at the power of the opposition, our
word is that of Elisha to his servant when the forces of the
king of Syria had surrounded Dothan: "Fear not; for they
that are with us are more than they that are with them." [9]

Our task is often to reveal the unseen allies of the spirit
of man. The feeling of utter helplessness in the face of giant
forces is characteristic of this time. Because we believe in
physical might whether it be in war or politics or business
or economic organization, we can see no place for the individual to assert himself in conflict with these forces. Where
shall a man find power to challenge all of these subhuman
influences which dwarf him and make him appear to be
utterly insignificant?

The preacher must still insist that each man's inner life
is a citadel which no power can invade without his consent.
God has not left us helpless and weak. The Christian knows
that God broke through into his life through Christ, to assure his victory over the principalities and powers against
which he must war. Let our message be a continual assurance
that God does intervene on man's side and that to our own
feeble attempts He lends a hand. People do not always know
consciously that they go to church to hear that assurance,
but they do. Very often, the preacher's most important function is to help a man go back into the arena of the world and
continue his battle against the powers of evil, with a renewed

---

[9] II Kings 6:16.

faith in unseen power and a new vision of the real meaning
of the contest.

Nowhere will the preacher need to associate himself with
his people more than here. Ours is not the task of standing
up above the battle, giving directions from the heights. We
are all in this together and we must help each other as we
fight for God. This is no fool's paradise we have wandered
into, but a battlefield where each man must make his choice
and take his place in the struggle. There are no spectators,
and the issues are life and death. Granted that mighty forces
are on the march and that a man can easily find reasons for
yielding to them. God does not allow us to be tempted beyond our power to resist, and He does not demand achievement beyond our strength. If there are great things to be
done, there is also great power available with which to do
them.

That which will endure the days ahead will be something
tough. If any man thinks the Gospel produces only sweet-
ness of character, let him study the lives of the saints. Those
who came out of the great tribulation were not mere observers who found their reward by keeping aloof from the
battle. In a time when many people shun the cross, and when
many sects spring up to tell people that "wishing will make
it so," preachers need to reveal that silly sentimental drivel
for what it is. We preach often to sick people who have made
ease the center of religion and to the spiritually emasculated
who seek an opiate.

If we are to preach power, we will have to preach theology.
The first-century preacher faced a generation that knew nothing about Christianity and needed to hear the great Christian doctrines proclaimed. More and more it seems to me
that one of the reasons his words struck fire, was because he
assumed that he was called to help men believe the right
things about God. Power is generated by great beliefs, and

in our attempt to be interesting and up to date we have too often neglected the powerhouse of our faith, which is its affirmations about how God works with men. No man will release power in his preaching, in my judgment, if he is "allergic to theology," as one of my friends put it.

David Grayson once said: "I wonder if ever you change human beings by arguments alone; either by peppering them with little sharp facts or by blowing them up with great guns of truth. You scare 'em, but do you change 'em?" Real religion is above argument because it goes deeper than the mind. Doctrinal preaching is not argumentative preaching, but witnessing to the Christian experience of having found the clue to abundant life. It is feeding the hunger for affirmations which Van Wyck Brooks said he found on every hand. Men want to be assured that the world can be changed and that it need not inevitably go back to the dark ages. They want to be assured that life can be better than is revealed by all the muck of advertising and vulgarity. They want to believe that God is and He speaks. What the early Christians did, we can do. We are able to affirm that these things are true, for the world has been changed for us, life has become better for us, and God speaks to us. The hunger to be something cannot be satisfied with little ethical homilies, but only by a kind of preaching whose roots are watered from the great reservoir of Christian doctrines.

Other ways of life endeavor to cover up the crises of life, while Christianity reveals them, uncovering the pain and suffering of the world. Is this wise? Not if men are unable to face the worst and conquer it. But Christianity's faith is that men are only half employed until they are faced with a situation proclaiming that for this cause they came into the world. Such an experience does not make a man small, for it drives him to God, whose power can then redeem his life.

I do not see how we can escape the implication that Christians are called upon to be better ethically than non-

Christians. The preacher ought to have the courage to say
this bluntly and say it often. There is always danger in making our religion merely a set of ethical principles, but there
is just as much danger in letting people forget that the best
missionary propaganda in the world is a life that is more
honest, more forgiving, more concerned with suffering than
other lives outside the Christian fellowship. The true sign
of the presence of a real Christian is not an ability to pray
or shout at a moment's notice, but a willingness to stand up
and be counted when a human value is at stake. We are
rightly warned against a mere activism that does not know
what God's long purposes are. But we had better proclaim
often that a Christian is one who does what God wants
done under all circumstances. It is for this that we are given
power.

The man who has had through the years a great purpose
to which he has given the best of his strength reveals it in his
face. Few things are more striking than this and harder to
describe. But the man who has found a work or a plan that
has engaged his best efforts has the look of strength and dignity. There is almost a kind of beauty even when the physical
appearance may deny it. In contrast to that kind of man, the
individual who has merely drifted without any effort to
withstand the current has an empty look with the passing
years. It is almost as if the soul had buried itself out of sight.
God redeems us by demanding the impossible, for out of
that demand comes the steadying discipline which keeps
our disorderly impulses under control.

Our evangelistic message is the word of power—power
enough for all our needs. The day is one of mass movements
and mighty forces, it is true, and they seem to dwarf the
individual. Yet the moving force is now and must always be
in personality. Movements begin in single persons, and God
still chooses men to work through, when He is letting loose
His power. In the face of the demonic forces, the preacher's

word is that even the demons are subject to Christ's power in us.

In all our groping for a method of evangelism, we still refuse to face the more fundamental problem of our lack of belief in the Gospel as the answer. Preaching is too much the creation of a mood favorable to the experiencing of nice, but vague, sentiments. But we are called to say to the people in the congregation that we know a way to be free from sin, to overcome temptation, and to conquer the world. If the Gospel is anything less than that, there is no method that will substitute for its ineffectiveness. But if it is all of that, and the preacher knows it and believes it, then the preached word will still penetrate into the heart with an irresistible demand to repent and be saved.

At the close of a preaching service, a young man came forward and said to the preacher: "I have been on the wrong track for three years. But if I dared to start on the right track, I didn't believe I could stay on it. Today you made me feel that if I made the decision, God would make me strong enough to keep it." Those simple words sum up the heart of our evangelistic message. "Even the youths shall faint and be weary"—that is true. "But they that wait upon the Lord" —to them shall be given power.

XI

A SERVANT OF THE CHURCH

". . . or despise ye the church of God?"

I Corinthians 11:22

Protestantism is always troubled when it comes to defining clearly its doctrine of the Church. Having turned away from the clear-cut authoritarian theory of Catholicism, and having put its emphasis on the priesthood of each believer, it finds it difficult not to regard the Church as anything more than another organization. Most of us feel that it must be more than that, but how to justify that something more is not always easy. In days when many people are hard put to see essential differences between the denominations, and when many people frankly shop around before deciding what church they will unite with in the new place, I sometimes envy my Catholic friends who belong to The Church, and that is that.

Great upheavals result in displacing millions of people. Out of that there is created a homesickness for a tradition that is sometimes, we must confess, no more than a vague ceremonial of a sick spirit. An urban, sophisticated civilization will turn to books that tell about a more simple, rural life. But the deep need for a sense of what happened in the past, and a feeling that we belong to something that did not begin with us and will not end with us, is always real. To keep the old things going and to push the new things along is one of those necessary tensions of life. It is the Church that must provide this, and Protestantism must find the way

209

to give its people the long look backward as well as the long
look forward.

We need to get more clearly the idea that the Church is
an essential part of the message. That is, the Christian message being what it is, the Church is an inevitable result of
it. This is not quite the same as insisting that a man cannot
have God for his Father unless he has the Church for his
mother, as St. Cyprian said. But it is to say that the Church
is a necessary part of the Christian revelation.

To the extent that Protestantism was a true reformation,
it became older than Catholicism. We need not feel that
we begin only with the sixteenth century, unless we assume
that at that time something new was started instead of something old recovered. Luther endeavored to go back of Con-
stantine and recover the truly Apostolic Church. When,
therefore, we are upbraided for not returning to the fold,
we can reply as did Dr. William P. Merrill of New York:
"If Roman Catholicism will constitute itself the elder brother
in the parable, then Protestantism will be perfectly willing
to constitute itself the younger brother, and both can come
back to the Fold." In the meantime, if we maintain our real
heritage, we are neither newer nor less certainly The Church
than any other group.

Certainly we shall not think of the Church as sinless or
of church members as supernatural. The Church is always
a perplexing combination of grandeur and scandal. The
Holy Spirit is not found always in the Church and it is never
found in the midst of bickering congregations. A pious,
sanctified selfishness is evil, perhaps more evil when it is
found within a church. There is a kind of extreme attitude
which assumes that in some strange way these things are
covered with a mantle of sanctity when they occur within
the Church. That, I do not believe.

But we cannot escape the certainty that the Church is a
miracle and a communication of God's grace. The preserva-

tion of Israel and the spread of Christianity, which are really one great event, proclaim God's presence in history. It is still true that we must judge the vine by the fruits. The Christian community, and before it the Jewish community, is one of the main fruits of our religion. Jesus did not organize the Church, but his teaching created the Church. There was never any doubt in the minds of men like St. Paul that the demonstration of the Gospel was in the fellowship of the Christian Church.

This Is the Church

In the preaching of the Gospel we need to bring people back to the divine aid which God gave the Church in its beginnings. Its emergence is one of those glorious things which tell us that God still protects His own. Its leader was killed, not in a respectable manner, but executed as a criminal. Celsus argued powerfully that a movement which endowed such a figure as the Galilean with divinity, and then insisted that redemption was revealed through him at a certain period of history, was a negation of the laws of nature, as indeed it was. Jesus left no successor and he had perfected no organized procedure. He wrote no book and the ethical teaching men remembered was simply impossible, the world being what it was. From the objective viewpoint, there was nothing to gain by becoming a Christian, and everything to lose. One lost social prestige and economic security, gaining in exchange the possibility of becoming a martyr.

There was no way to tell where the demands of the teaching would stop. Give it an inch, and it seemed to take a mile. As early as 119, it is recorded that Hermes, a prefect of Rome, freed 1,250 slaves after having had them baptized into his own faith. Not all the early Christians did that, but, there being no set limits to the demands of this religion, worldly wise men could see that the only safe thing was to stay out of it altogether. Yet in spite of the denial of prudence, the Church found men willing to die for its Gospel.

As soon as it became apparent that the purposes of the Church could never be brought under the control of the government (as was true of the other tolerated religions), persecution began in earnest. The issue was defined by Tertullian when he said:

> I refuse to call the Emperor a god. If he is human, it behooves him as such to bow the knee to God. Augustus, the founder of the Empire, was reluctant to be addressed even as Lord (dominus), and this, indeed, is an appellation of God. I am willing to call the Emperor Lord but only in the conventional sense, never in the sense in which I accord that title to the Omnipotent and Eternal who is his Lord as well as mine.[1]

Perhaps the first five hundred years were the worst, and to have come through that period was a sign that something had happened that would henceforth have to be taken into account.

The toughness of the Church is not something apparent to outsiders; men all the way from Nero to Hitler have assumed that it could be destroyed, or at least silenced, whenever it became a stumbling block to their own plans. Compared to the obvious power of the state or the army, the Church appears to be utterly helpless. But it is discovered that there is something in it upheld by the universe, and its foundations go down to the absolutes of life. How difficult it is to kill a church, or even to merge it with another. The organization may be struggling and apparently unable to maintain itself another year, but when some well-meaning official tries to mercifully apply the final blow, it refuses to die.

I attended a church anniversary one time, and listened

---

1 Quoted by Cochrane, *Christianity and Classical Culture,* Oxford, 1940, 227.

to its history read by one of the elders. It was a story of fore-
closures, of unbearable financial burdens, of schisms, and of
hopeless debts. As I listened to the frank story of the past, I
said to myself, "Only a church could have endured it and
lived." The wonder is not that the Church often falls on
evil days, but that it has managed to exist at all, let alone
grow. When Disraeli was asked what proof he had of God,
he replied, "The Jews." And to the man who asks what proof
there is of the Gospel's power, we might reply: "The Church."

There is something about Jesus that finds men even when
they try to escape him. There is something about his teach-
ings that exercise a mighty fascination even when they seem
to repel, and in spite of all our denials and pretensions, everything that is good in us responds to him. The Church of
Christ shares his nature to the extent that when it is most
derided, it can no more be toppled over than Jesus can be
destroyed.

The Church is supported by voluntary contributions. How
many societies are there to which each member gives what
he is able or willing to give? No other organization would
dare undertake a tremendous missionary enterprise, launch
great social programs, promise maintenance for a huge number of professional workers all on the basis of voluntary
contributions. A man said to Carlyle: "Did you know that
Christianity is on its last legs?" To which Carlyle replied:
"Christianity is always on its last legs." At least, any generation that decided the Church was not worth supporting
could end the whole enterprise. Always it seems to be pre-
cariously near to destruction, but it lives and it grows, because it is tough.

The Church is unique in that it belongs to two worlds,
and is a creature of a divine dimension as well as of a human
one. It is the creator of tension in society, and of its life it
might be said, "The Church comes to bring not peace, but
a sword." It is never quite at ease in its political relations.

It can never be just a creature of the state, existing to maintain the morale of the government. It stands in judgment
over all society. Yet it cannot solve the dilemma by becoming
the government itself, and the times when it has been led
into this path were tragic for the Church and for society. The
medieval Church created a unified society, and that was
good, but it was corrupted by power, and that was evil. The
relation between Church and state is therefore always an
uneasy one because the lines cannot be drawn and the spheres
defined. All of life belongs to God and hence it is of concern
to the Church, but temporal power transforms the Church
from being a part of the healing to becoming a part of the
disease.

Canon Cocklin of St. Paul's Cathedral, London, wrote: "I
believe the Christian Church to be the one hope of salvation
for the individual and the community, and I regard it at the
moment as itself one of the greatest obstacles to the achievement of its own true aim." When Eusebius pointed to the
triumph of the Church over the empire as evidence that
God approved of it, he suggested the dangerous error that
Christianity is a success cult. When it accepts that viewpoint,
then it is indeed the chief obstacle in the way of its own
true aim.

George Bernard Shaw was commenting on one of his con-
temporaries who had resigned his seat in Parliament rather
than compromise his principle.

When I think of my own unfortunate character [he said],
smirched with compromise, rotted with opportunism, mil-
dewed with expediency, blackened by ink contributed to
Tory and Liberal newspapers, dragged through the mud of
Borough Councils and Battersea elections, stretched out of
shape with wire pulling, putrefied by permeation, worn out
by twenty-five years' pushing to gain an inch here and straining
to stem a backrush there, I do think Joe might have put up
with just a speck or two on those white robes of his for the
sake of the millions of poor devils who cannot afford any char-

acter at all because they have no friends in parliament. Oh, these moral dandies, these spiritual toffs! These superior persons! Who is Joe anyhow that he should not risk his soul occasionally like the rest of us?

This is what the Church has to do. It must be down in the dirt and the filth, but it must also live on the peaks. So there is a sense in which you can only speak of the Church in paradoxes, and when you give only one aspect, you are speaking the truth, but also the lie. It is this unique double nature of the Church that must be understood, though it is often very confusing to the uninitiated.

We must realize that the Church is a necessity and not a free option. There are great numbers of people talking about the need for a spiritual awakening in the world, but not many people are doing anything about it. Yet, if we give any serious consideration to the matter, we know that it takes an organization to unite men in a common purpose and to accomplish changes in society. Let us say to this generation: To whom, then, will you go, you well-meaning people who are worried over the direction we move? Where will you throw your influence and your energy to halt the disintegration? What will revitalize our life? Will the patriotic societies, the service clubs, the lodges, or the social welfare groups do it? Hardly! Will a kind of vague, individual religion do it? Not unless history reverses itself, for the saints have all come out of a tradition, and never did they find nourishment for their lives in a vacuum.

If the new power of faith is to become effective, it will not be out of the cry from isolated voices expressing a sense of need. It will be done by groups of people who can create a redeemed fellowship within the present situation. The past would have been quite different if the forces of darkness could have dealt with men separately, but it was another story when they had to deal with the Church. It was the Church that brought light out of darkness and order out

of chaos. It was the Church that salvaged the achievement
of Rome. It should not be forgotten that when the Visigoths
sacked Rome in 410, they spared the churches because Ul-
filas had been among them with the word of Christ, and
they were already partly Christianized. In every great crisis
during the last nineteen hundred years it has been the
Church that was a bulwark of strength. It is hard to see how
any individual can cry out for a spiritual rebirth of our
civilization, and then justify standing apart from the one
institution that is trying to do something about it.

Even those forces which have won what seemed like overwhelming victories over the Church have had a curious feeling of uncertainty within them. They seem to be always
insistent that full credit be given them for their accomplishments. "Look at what we have done," they seem to say. "The
Church has been silenced and shackled. This time it is for
ever and we are triumphant at last. Rejoice with us and
give us your full confidence." But the more they insist, the
more they reveal their own inner insecurity and the haunt-
ing suspicion that their very victories are in some mad
fashion steps toward disaster. The Church is astounding
in that it can afford defeats, for it can use them as foundation stones for its own future victory. Perhaps there is no
better indication that it partakes of the ultimate nature of
things.

Growth and Influence

The victory of the Church over the barbarians was in a
sense too great. It was unequal to wielding so much power
without becoming corrupt. The revolt against it was a revolt
for freedom from an intolerable control. But as is so often
the case, the revolt went too far and the cure became the
source of a worse disease. For in the enthusiasm of the Renaissance, the prevailing spirit isolated nature from God and
unduly magnified man. It made absolutes of culture and

civilization and deified freedom. The disunity of Christendom was one of the unfortunate results.

But that period beginning with the Reformation was the period of the Evangelical Revival in England which set in motion waves of social reform which have never stopped. It was the period of America's birth and growth with its great experiment in democracy affecting the thought and imagination of the whole world. That experiment rested on Christian principles announced and maintained by the Church. It was the period of the developing of education, first started by the Church. It was the period of the missionary movement, which for magnitude, amount of money invested, and people involved has never been equaled. In a day when many people were isolationist because they never traveled beyond their own land, the Church went into all the world. Today we can affirm that there has never been a time when the Church extended over so wide a territory as right now, and there never has been a time when the Church was in a position to exercise so much influence.

It is this continued growth that has escaped so many people. The waves of its progress have mounted higher each time. If some person says that the Church is dying and at the end, then let it be said: "The burden of proof is on you, and on the basis of the past you are wrong." It is not for churchmen to be on the defensive.

It has been a common criticism of Protestants that they do not know what they believe. There is some justification for the criticism, though we are not going to heal our diseases by bringing back the catechism to our Sunday Schools or by teaching adults to repeat theological statements of what they are supposed to believe. Just now I think it is more important that Protestants should be made more aware of the great sweep of that fellowship to which they belong. We hear a note here and a note there, but too few churchmen are acquainted with the whole symphony of the Christian Church.

It seems to me to be as important to know what we belong to, as to know what we believe. When one hears the boasting about relatively unimportant little groups, one wonders why a member of the Church does not shout from the house-tops his pride in this greatest of all institutions. Preachers will do well to preach at least one series of sermons a year on the Church.

Gibbon wrote in his famous *History of the Decline and Fall of the Roman Empire:* "I have written of the victory of Barbarism and Religion." The modern historian, how-ever, has developed a blind spot which prevents him from seeing the influence of religion anywhere. It is amazing to see the number of histories written that give the Church scarcely a footnote. Yet, if any man takes the time to study as objec-tively as possible the history of the West during the past nineteen centuries, he is astounded at the difference Chris-tianity has made. Its social influence has been mediated through the Church.

One could talk about public morals, amusements, and cus-toms, or prison reform, ministries to the sick and the poor, or social ethics. Everywhere there is the hand of the Church. The great abolitionist movement was begun by the Quaker John Woolman's being troubled in his conscience when asked to make out a bill of sale for one of his employer's slaves. H. G. Wells said in his *Outline of History* that labor owes more to the Church than to any other organization for a growing recognition of its rights and dignity. One need not assume the role of an apologist to make abundantly clear that when the ledger is balanced, our civilization owes most of all to the Church, in spite of the fact that it has sometimes been a stumbling block to progress. No part of our life has been able to maintain itself outside the influence of our Christianity. It is not merely a coincidence that a generation that loses its sense of obligation to the Church begins to lose its power of self-determination.

Through Suffering to World Fellowship

If anyone had told us ten years ago that Christians would ever again have to go through experiences of persecution like those the first Christian centuries endured, most of us would have thought such talk grossly exaggerated. Yet this is precisely what happened in lands under the domination of the Nazis and the Japanese militarists. The Book of Revelation came back into its own and we began to understand such phrases as "the beast." Men who were called on to die for their faith were no longer legendary heroes but contemporary figures. Twentieth-century Christians have their own martyrologies.[2]

We were thrilled by the stories from Norway telling about all but twenty-seven pastors resigning rather than taking orders from a tyrant. More times than not it was a village priest or pastor who represented the element in Norwegian life that could not be conquered. The French Church found a new power and French Christians made great sacrifices to help their more unfortunate brethren and to maintain chaplains in German prison camps. German Christians had men like Niemöller and Archbishop Galen to bring back the spirit of Martin Luther. Christians in the Netherlands associated themselves with their Jewish brethren to share their shame and suffering. Such was the record that Albert Einstein confessed his admiration for the Church he had once despised.

The Christian Church still resists. The very word "Protestant" speaks of this important function; the protesting of the Church has been one of its greatest services. It is wonderful how often the Church sees the trend toward dehumanization before any other group is aware of it, and how, under its leadership, such policies are challenged and stopped. We are not always brave, but the most realistic

---

[2] I have used Van Dusen's *What Is the Church Doing?* (Scribner's, 1943) for much of this.

thinking about society is done within the Church because it knows best the real nature of man. It is still true that the center of resistance to injustice, greed, and discriminations is the Church.

There is resolution in the Church. When once the issue is defined and the nature of the conflict apparent, then it draws a line beyond which it will not retreat. Someone is reported to have said at an important conference some time ago that the Church must be careful not to sponsor any more lost causes. But the past reveals that no one can be sure about a lost cause and no one can define it with accuracy. The Church when it is at its best is never afraid of what the world calls "lost causes." It has not been afraid to experience failure, and in its hours of failure, its faith has been reborn. Wendell Willkie said one time that all a man needs to get on in the world is a powerful enemy. It is hardly too much to say that the Church has been its best under the heavy blows of its enemies—the world, the flesh, and the devil.

On that fateful September 3, 1939, when England declared war on Germany, the Christian Church established on every continent faced one of its most severe testings. Would it become a collection of national groups, each praying for the destruction of its enemies, among whom there would certainly be many Christians? The Church made some serious errors, but in the main it stood the test. The world organization of the Church proved its ability to withstand the strains of war and maintain its world-wide fellowship. Orphaned missions were taken over by other groups and supported. British Christians gave generously to this cause in the dark days of 1940, one of the most critical moments in the nation's history. Faculty and student body of the Central China College, after fleeing westward with what equipment they could carry, took an offering for Christians suffering in the London Blitz.

When the so-called realists tell us that we cannot have

world fellowship, the Church can reply: "We have created one." In the midst of the cynical weariness which has overwhelmed so many idealists, we have something which points the way to the possibility of one world. We have failed to rightly estimate the success already attained by the Church in establishing a supernational fellowship. It is one of the new, creative forces in a disintegrating world. It is the surest sign that God is still with us.

It is important to remember that the international fellowship was not the first aim of the Christian missionaries. That is, they did not go forth with the primary object of bridging cultures, or interpreting nationalities to each other. They went forth to tell the good news of Christianity to as many people as they could reach. Their assumption was that they knew something that every man, because he was a man, needed to hear. As a matter of fact, in recent times at least, there has been considerable criticism of the whole missionary enterprise because so many of those involved in it were unaware of international relations and cultural backgrounds.

In all of this, let us not lose sight of a very important thing. The world fellowship is an effect and not a cause. It is one of the fruits of Christianity rather than its root. Any attempt to build the fellowship apart from the Christian doctrines and beliefs will be in vain. The Church is a fellowship of *believers*. Too many people assume that peace is something you can have by agreements and treaties, or through right-thinking diplomats working out the arrangements. The truth is that peace rests on justice which interpenetrates life whenever one man is in relation to another. So the world fellowship rests upon and is helpless without individual Christians who hold to certain fundamentals of their faith, and live their lives on the basis of those fundamentals. There is no way to hurry the coming of the Kingdom, and it waits for enough men who are capable of holding it up. And they must be men who have accepted the Christian belief about God, man, history, and charted their behavior in the light of those affirmations.

Christian unity finds its basis in the essentials of the faith. Too often we have been guilty, like Don Quixote, of fighting windmills, imagining them to be real enemies. Forms of worship or organizations are only secondary matters. The safeguarding of the ministry from careless, unworthy, unsanctified persons is important, but any mechanical theory of choosing men is little better than superstition. Our definitions of what is holy, change. Remember that Samuel Gorton was banished from Plymouth because he was found guilty of defending his maid, who had smiled in church.

But the only kind of tolerance that is worth anything at all is based on beliefs that are held with tenacity and sincerity. An easygoing liberalism always promises more immediate results in the way of unity, but the promise is a false one. The first tempest blows down any house built on it. A man like Wesley, who at the age of eighty-five could invite into his societies men of many differing opinions, was being truly tolerant. For he held to what seemed to him the essential things in the Gospel, without any compromise. Only a tolerance built on convictions is in harmony with the spirit of Jesus.

We are in danger of overemphasizing the weaknesses of difference. Much can be said about the scandal of our Protestant divisions and our useless quarrels. It is true that we could save money on overhead expenses if we had but one organization. There are times when we stand powerless in the face of a great danger or a great opportunity. But the answer is not necessarily a single organization.

It is about time that we become suspicious of any organization that is too big. I doubt if the world is going to be a happier place to live in, now that there are only three superstates, instead of a score or more of sovereign nations. Our cities get beyond a certain size and their efficiency declines with every added unit of population. In business, we pay at least a lip service to the preservation of small business in the face of the threat of giant monopolies. The war taught us that there are important values in decentralization.

Nature does not seem to put much stress on 100 per cent this or that. Mixtures seem to be quite welcome in the natural order, and the purely bred animals often turn out to be little better than idiots. Variety seems to mean health as well as interest. We do not work pure gold or pure iron. Our meals would get tiresome if they were 100 per cent cake.

The Church needs differences, but it does not want competitions within itself, nor can it be the Church with bickerings and jealousies raging between denominations. But if we can find our unity against the pagan world within our variations, then Protestantism can be truly The Church. In spite of apparent disunities, which often are not real, it is still the Church alone among human institutions that stands for the universal brotherhood of man and the unity of the human race.

Implications

It is well to keep in mind the vital relationship between preaching and the Church, for it was preaching, under God, that brought the Church into being. The preacher needs to remind himself that his position as a representative of the Church has become a wider one with the years. Today he speaks in the name of a supernational, super-racial institution that is no longer a dream but a reality. It is not to be despised or belittled, but held before the world in all its divine grandeur.

The important part played by preaching on the great rebirths of the Church becomes apparent to any man who studies the past. The simple preaching of the Franciscans to the poor was one of the significant chapters in the history of the Church. The period before the Reformation saw preaching reach such a sad decline that religion became mostly a matter of pagan ceremonies, pilgrimages, and penances. The decline of preaching is always a decline of the Church, and, among other things, the Reformation was the restoration of preaching to its rightful place.

In the Scots' Confession of 1560, the true Church is characterized as a place where the true preaching of the Word of God takes place. The Thirty-Nine Articles of 1571 made it clear that the Church and preaching are to be held together. Methodists have inherited that doctrine in their Articles of Religion:

> The visible Church of Christ is a congregation of faithful men in which the pure Word of God is preached, and the Sacraments duly administered according to Christ's ordinance, in all those things that of necessity are requisite to the same. (Article XIII)

The Wesleyan Revival in eighteenth-century England was a new emphasis placed on lay preaching. Whenever we think of the Oxford Movement, we think of Newman in the pulpit of St. Mary's.

If we were to prophesy concerning the future on the basis of the Church's experience in the past, we would say that the revival of the Church must always wait for, or be accomplished by, the revival of preaching. The new Church, able to deal with the power problems of the new day, must have prophetic leaders, preachers above all. Lectures in the pulpit or secularized homilies will never do it, but we must have sermons which proclaim and interpret the Good News that God through Christ has bequeathed to us. The past tells of the inability of any method or approach to take the place of the preaching of the Word.

The preacher must think of himself always as a servant of the Church. It is never an organization set up to provide for him a pulpit and a group of listeners. Paul attacks the

Corinthian Christians for making the Lord's Supper a drunken feast, and he seeks to bring them to their senses by pointing out that such action is to despise the Church of God. When the Sacrament became a means to some selfish end, then, says the Apostle, that brings shame to the Church. Even so, when a man uses the sacrament of preaching as something for his own personal aggrandizement, that too brings shame to the Church.

A preacher sometimes speaks of the church where he ministers as "my church." Outsiders fall into the same habit and refer to a church as "Dr. Blank's church." Often this is quite harmless and done without any thought of turning the local institution over to an individual. Yet it contains a serious danger in that a man may begin to think in terms of his ownership of the church and his right to administer it to suit his own convenience. Any of the dogmatic professions carry this danger of putting oneself above the institution. Let the preacher say over and over again, "I am the servant of the Church."

There is sometimes a temptation to show a false courage in the pulpit rather than minister to the people. It is still possible to become seekers after martyrdom and thus receive a certain satisfaction even when the Church itself may be split apart. We are not called upon to compromise principles for the sake of the institution, but we are expected to speak our truth in love. Our ministry is the Church's ministry and it is most effective when it has been able to speak through the unity of the Christian fellowship. To go by ourselves and to speak for ourselves is often spectacular and brilliant, but the Kingdom of God is best served when the preacher can lift his people to a higher plane within the community.

The preacher is also a teacher as well as a prophet. The prophet had no continuing congregation, but most of us will be speaking to the same people many times a year. Our task, therefore, is not to make a scintillating impression week after week, as indeed few men can do anyway. But it is to hold the tension of the Gospel over against each man's life. If we are servants of the Church we will learn how to submerge our egos and consecrate them to the larger fellowship.

On the other hand, the servant of the Church must not assume that he is commissioned to preach "peace, peace, when there is no peace." The preacher is not to keep harmony within the Church at the expense of the Christian witness. Much of the hostility against the Church comes from those who have watched it side with the powers of the *status quo,* while robed men stood in the pulpits counseling contentment. The real servant of the Church would have been urging rebellion and stabbing the saints awake with God's divine discontent. There are worse things than conflict, and the man who feels his ministry has been a success because he has escaped controversy by refusing to raise a single moral issue is a despoiler of the Church and not its servant.

A few simple principles will help the preacher to bring the Church through a controversial question, if not with perfect agreement, at least without bitterness. Always begin on a common ground and have some kind of proposition to which all may assent. Do not begin with the assumption that people are going to disagree and then proceed to champion one side with arguments. Avoid labels and use comparisons in the accepted realms of thinking. Always end on a high, positive note. The pulpit is the freest platform in the world, and most congregations will let a man speak his word if he does it with courtesy and tact, as is befitting one who respects and serves his congregation.

It has been estimated that the American Church has wealth to the extent of about $2,700,000.[3] An institution that has given such hostages to fortune had better remember its Lord's warning that where your treasure is, there will your heart

---

[3] Babson, Zuver, *Can These Bones Live?* Harper, 1945, 87.

be also. The temptation of the preacher will be to risk
nothing that will jeopardize the Church's holdings. Thus, it
is not an easy thing to be a servant of the Church. It demands both love and courage. It demands preachers who
have developed the single eye centered on God, and willing
to make any personal sacrifice, just so the Church realizes
its divine function.

There are men who are afraid of their congregations, and
the deacons soon learn about it and make it miserable for
him. To such men let it be said that the congregation is not
a monster or a baby or a colossus. It is a man to be dealt
with as you deal with men. If God has called us to preach,
then we ought to believe that He has called the congregation to share with us in the work of the Church. Since it is
His work and we are all partners in it together, fear is only
the sign of an unwillingness to surrender our egotism to Him.

Because we are sometimes afraid of people, we are out of
touch with them. We cannot even tell when we are boring
them. There is a story about a sexton who slipped a note
on the pulpit which read: "When you are through the sermon, please put out the lights and lock the church." We
must know our congregations so well that through them we
shall know humanity. We must know what they are reading
and how they are being amused. What do they do with their
leisure and how do they spend their time when they are
not working? If this knowledge is sometimes disturbing, we
must have it in order to speak to their need.

Henry James once suggested that the test of a novel is
whether or not it arouses the emotion of surprise or recognition. The same thing might be said of the sermon. Preachers do not exist to tell people what they never knew, but
to show them their own hearts. John Wesley wrote in his
Journal September 6, 1743, concerning a preaching experience in Cornwall: "But still I could not find the way into
the hearts of the hearers." And no man has truly preached

until that has been done, but it will not be done until he knows his people and loves them.

Richard Baxter used to say that he preached over his people's heads once a year to show them what he could do every Sunday if he chose. This is much better than preaching down to our congregations. One of the most alarming things is the ignorance of the average churchgoer concerning the Bible, theology, and the history of the Church. No preacher has done his duty who has not made his ministry an informing one and helped to create intelligent churchmen through the years. Joseph Noyes, minister of First Church, New Haven, excused his shallow sermons because of the ignorance of Yale students. President Clap replied that as long as they had to listen to such preaching, they would always be ignorant. One of our chief functions is to get people to think, and it is lack of thought that represents danger to the Church. The demagogue may speak in a manner to appeal to the mob, but we speak to the Church.

Not always will the people believe the preacher, but they must always believe *in* the preacher. And the preacher must always believe in the people. Even when there is a lovelessness in the Church that makes his preaching like sounding brass, still he must believe that the Word can soften the hearts of hardened church members. The glory of the Church is that it accepts men without reference to any special status, and it becomes, therefore, not an aristocratic organization but the meeting place of men. Any church that tries to make itself a class institution will find, just as does the drama, that such procedure is failure. The man who can speak to only a special class is no true messenger of Christ.

To the preacher who is willing to pay the price, there is released great power. When the long preparation has been made, the careful study protected, the pastoral work undertaken, and the life yielded to God, then come the words to change lives. With tenderness the preacher brings healing to the sorrowful and with assurance he brings triumph to the warriors of Christ. But for these great gifts, he must give a strict account. He can so easily come to believe that the brilliance of his personal performance is an end in itself. Such a man does not carry a church with him nor give its life any permanent enrichment.

To some extent, the measure of a man's ministry is what happens to the church after he leaves it. It should not be necessary to say that if there is an unforgivable sin in the ministry, it is to keep coming back to a church where you have previously served. The man who in any way interferes with the ministry of his successor is beneath our contempt. The sooner we can make up our minds that our retirement will not be a meddling nuisance to the next man's pastoral relationships, the better for us, for him, and for the Church.

But even if we escape these grosser sins, we shall be judged if our work has not been of lasting worth. The Church cannot be constantly starting over with every new minister. It must have the sense of a continuing ministry, which is possible when preachers bring men into a devoted loyalty to the Church and not to themselves. The real preacher rejoices from the depth of his heart when his people give the same love to his successor that they gave to him. Then he can be sure that he did his work well. For let us never forget that preaching is not the activity of a single individual, but an act of the Church, and it leads men to Christ through the fellowship of the Church.

INDEX